Flask Web Development

"A Beginner's Guide to Mastering Flask for Web Applications"

Joseph Scott

© **Copyright 2023 - All rights reserved.**

The contents of this book may not be reproduced, duplicated or transmitted without direct written permission from the author.

Under no circumstances will any legal responsibility or blame be held against the publisher for any reparation, damages, or monetary loss due to the information herein, either directly or indirectly.

Legal Notice:
This book is copyright protected. This is only for personal use. You cannot amend, dis-tribute, sell, use, quote or paraphrase any part or the content within this book without the consent of the author.

Disclaimer Notice:
Please note the information contained within this document is for educational and entertainment purposes only. Every attempt has been made to provide accurate, up to date and reliable complete information. Readers acknowledge that the author is not engaging in the rendering of legal, financial, medical or professional advice. The content of this book has been derived from various sources. Please consult a licensed professional before attempting any techniques outlined in this book.

By reading this document, the reader agrees that under no circumstances is the author responsible for any losses, direct or indirect, which are incurred as a result of the use of information contained within this document.

Table of Contents

Introduction 4

Chapter One: Getting Started with Flask 14

Chapter Two: Routing and Views 25

Chapter Three: Templates and Static Files 36

Chapter Four: Forms and User Input 47

Chapter Five: Databases in Flask 58

Chapter Six: User Authentication 70

Chapter Seven: Flask Extensions 82

Chapter Eight: Building RESTful APIs 94

Chapter Nine: Error Handling and Debugging 106

Chapter Ten: Testing Your Flask Application 118

Chapter Eleven: Deploying Flask Applications 130

Chapter Twelve: Best Practices for Flask Development 144

Chapter Thirteen: Beyond the Basics 156

Conclusion 168

Introduction

Overview of Flask and its place in web development

In the web development landscape, Flask emerges as a Python-based micro-framework known for its straightforward, adaptable, and user-centric design. It is an optimal platform for developers planning to execute a variety of web-related projects, from basic web interfaces to intricate, expandable web platforms. This narrative sheds light on Flask's unique role in web development, spotlighting its essential attributes, philosophical underpinnings, and its adaptability to a range of project requirements.

At its foundation, Flask is bolstered by the Werkzeug WSGI toolkit and the Jinja2 template engine. Werkzeug serves as a bridge to the Web Server Gateway Interface (WSGI), a standard ensuring seamless interaction between web servers and applications, while Jinja2 offers a potent templating language for the dynamic generation of web content, thus neatly separating the business logic from the presentation layer. This dual foundation affords developers both the flexibility and efficiency necessary for crafting web applications.

The term 'micro' in Flask's description speaks to its philosophy of keeping the core streamlined yet expandable. It offers just the essentials needed to get a web application off the ground, without mandating the use of specific tools or libraries. This minimalist philosophy allows developers the freedom to pick and choose the tools that best fit their project's needs, highlighting Flask's versatility.

Flask's API is noted for its clarity and straightforwardness, making the development process approachable for novices yet robust enough for experienced developers to undertake sophisticated projects. Flask fosters the creation of applications that are both scalable and easy to maintain, in line with the best practices in web development.

A standout feature of Flask is its elegant routing system, enabling developers to easily link URLs to Python functions, which is key to creating neat, RESTful web services. This ease of use extends to Flask's handling of requests, responses, form data, and cookies, offering a straightforward interface to the HTTP protocol.

Despite its simplicity, Flask boasts considerable power, capable of being scaled up through the use of extensions that introduce additional functionalities like database integration, authentication systems, and session management. This rich ecosystem of extensions allows for the integration of sophisticated features without weighing down the framework.

Flask's adaptability makes it an excellent choice for a wide spectrum of web development endeavors, from smaller projects and prototypes that benefit from quick development turns to more sizable applications, given the appropriate architecture and extensions. Flask's ability to work seamlessly with other Python libraries and services makes it a favored option for crafting microservices, APIs, and web services that require high levels of performance and scalability.

The Flask community is another pillar of its strength, with an active and engaged base contributing to the framework's enhancement and offering an extensive array of resources, documentation, tutorials, and plugins. This enriches the learning experience and speeds up the development process.

Compared to other web frameworks, Flask is distinguished by its minimalist and modular approach, offering developers a clean slate to custom-build applications without the burden of unnecessary features, unlike more comprehensive frameworks such as Django.

Flask's lightweight nature and accessible entry point also make it particularly suitable for educational settings, where it serves as a tool for demystifying web development concepts in a digestible format.

To sum up, Flask epitomizes a seamless blend of simplicity, flexibility, and strength in the domain of web development. Its minimalist yet extensible approach renders it a versatile toolkit for a broad array of web applications, providing a sturdy, scalable base that empowers developers to efficiently bring their creative visions to fruition. Flask's enduring relevance and appeal in the dynamic field of web development are ensured by its straightforward and effective framework.

What you will learn from this book

Diving into "Flask Web Development: A Beginner's Guide to Mastering Flask for Web Applications" offers an expansive learning experience for both new and experienced developers.

This guide meticulously navigates through the extensive capabilities of Flask in crafting web applications, presenting a rich curriculum designed to imbue readers with a profound understanding of Flask's functionalities and best practices.

From the onset, the guide lays a solid foundation by introducing Flask's architecture and guiding principles, ensuring readers grasp the underlying concepts that drive its design. This foundational knowledge is pivotal, enabling informed decision-making throughout the development process and instilling a commitment to adhering to best practices from the start.

Progressing through the guide, readers are taken on a deep dive into Flask's routing and view mechanisms, essential for the backbone of web applications. This section empowers readers to adeptly map URLs to Python functions and devise dynamic routes, crucial for creating intuitive web interfaces. Beyond technical implementation, emphasis is placed on writing clean, maintainable code, a hallmark of professional development practices.

The exploration extends to templates and static files, where readers become proficient with the Jinja2 templating engine. Through practical exercises, the guide teaches how to render dynamic content responsive to user interactions and application states, going beyond syntax to cover best practices in template structure and static asset management.

Handling user input is a critical component of web applications, thoroughly addressed in this guide. Readers will navigate the complexities of form handling in Flask, mastering data collection, complex validation, and processing techniques. The discussions also cover vital security practices, including CSRF protection and secure data handling, underscoring the guide's commitment to robust web security education.

Database integration is demystified, guiding readers through the intricacies of Flask-SQLAlchemy. This section is invaluable for those aiming to build data-centric applications, offering insights into effective data modeling, transaction management, and optimization for performance.

The guide also tackles user authentication and session management comprehensively. Readers are equipped to implement secure authentication systems, manage user sessions effectively, and protect applications against prevalent security threats, an indispensable skill set for any web application developer.

Beyond core functionalities, the guide delves into the vast ecosystem of Flask extensions, providing insights into not only their integration but also the mechanics behind them. This knowledge is essential for enhancing Flask applications and troubleshooting complex issues.

API development with Flask is another critical area covered, equipping readers with the skills to design and implement RESTful APIs that adhere to security, versioning, and documentation best practices, a skill set increasingly relevant in today's microservices and mobile backend development landscapes.

Error handling and debugging are addressed with the depth and clarity they warrant, teaching readers to construct resilient error management systems and employ effective debugging techniques to swiftly resolve issues, enhancing overall user experience.

The guide places significant emphasis on testing, introducing readers to automated testing practices within Flask. This section covers everything from unit tests to integration tests and test-driven development, ensuring the reliability and maintainability of applications.

Concluding with deployment, the guide demystifies the process, presenting various platforms and strategies to transition applications from development to production seamlessly, preparing readers for real-world deployment challenges.

In essence, "Flask Web Development: A Beginner's Guide to Mastering Flask for Web Applications" is more than just a book; it's an immersive educational journey through Flask's web development landscape. It aims to equip readers not only with the skills to build web applications but also with a deep understanding of utilizing Flask to tackle complex development challenges, making it an invaluable resource for anyone aspiring to excel in web development with Flask.

Setting up your development environment

Creating a conducive development environment is a pivotal first step in any web development endeavor, especially when embarking on projects using Flask, a renowned Python-based micro-framework celebrated for its simplicity and effectiveness. Establishing this environment involves a meticulous setup of various tools, software, and workflows that collectively ensure a seamless, efficient, and collaborative development process. This detailed exposition aims to delineate the essential elements and practices for configuring a comprehensive development setup tailored for Flask-based projects.

1. Operating System Selection

The operating system (OS) choice can greatly influence the ease of development and compatibility with various tools. While Flask's adaptable nature allows it to function across Windows, macOS, and Linux, the latter two, with their Unix-based command lines, are often favored for Python-centric development and server-side deployments. Windows users can bridge this gap by utilizing the Windows Subsystem for Linux (WSL), offering a comparable development experience.

2. Python Setup

Given that Flask is built atop Python, a proper Python environment is indispensable. Utilizing version management tools like `pyenv` for Linux/macOS or its Windows counterpart `pyenv-win` facilitates managing multiple Python versions, allowing for smooth project transitions. Ensuring accessible Python and `pip` installations from the command line is crucial for unimpeded development.

3. Employing Virtual Environments

Virtual environments are fundamental in Python development, providing isolated spaces to manage project-specific dependencies and avoid conflicts. Utilizing `venv` or `**virtualenv**` for creating these environments ensures that each project has its dedicated library set, independent of the global Python setup.

4. Development Tools and Editors

The choice of an Integrated Development Environment (IDE) or code editor is subjective but pivotal, with a preference for those offering robust Python support. Options like PyCharm, Visual Studio Code (VS Code), and Sublime Text are popular, equipped with features such as syntax highlighting, auto-completion, and debugging tailored for Python and Flask, enhanced further by Flask-specific plugins.

5. Implementing Version Control

In contemporary development workflows, a version control system like Git is indispensable for managing code versions, facilitating team collaborations, and tracking changes. Platforms such as GitHub, GitLab, or Bitbucket provide not just repository hosting but also tools for code review, issue tracking, and CI/CD pipelines, essential for streamlined development and deployment.

6. Managing Dependencies

Maintaining project stability and ensuring reproducibility demands effective dependency management. While **pip** alongside a `**requirements.txt**` file can manage dependencies, tools like `**Pipenv**` or `**Poetry**` offer advanced dependency resolution and environment management, including lock files for consistent installations.

7. Configuring Development Servers and Debugging

Flask's in-built development server offers convenience for local testing, including features like hot reloading and interactive debugging. For more comprehensive debugging, IDEs like PyCharm or VS Code extensions provide an integrated debugging experience with functionalities like breakpoints and variable inspections.

8. Database Configuration

Data persistence setups vary widely across web projects, necessitating a tailored database setup. Flask's compatibility with databases from SQLite to more complex systems like PostgreSQL or MySQL allows for flexible data management solutions. Docker can be particularly useful here, containerizing databases for consistent, hassle-free setup across environments.

9. Code Quality Assurance

Ensuring code quality and consistency is critical, especially in collaborative settings. Integrating linters like `**flake8**` and formatters like `**black**` into the development environment helps enforce coding standards and styles, often supported by automatic linting and formatting features in many IDEs and editors.

10. Setting Up Testing Frameworks

A robust testing setup is integral to the development lifecycle, underpinning the reliability and functionality of the codebase. Flask's compatibility with testing extensions and standard Python testing frameworks like `**unittest**` and `**pytest**` facilitates a culture of test-driven development (TDD) and smooth integration into CI processes.

11. Documentation Practices

As projects scale, comprehensive and up-to-date documentation becomes vital. Tools like Sphinx, which integrates seamlessly with Flask, enable the generation of detailed documentation, ensuring that both current and future developers can easily navigate and contribute to the project.

12. Incorporating CI/CD Practices

Embedding CI/CD tools into the development environment enhances deployment efficiency and code integration reliability. Platforms like Jenkins, Travis CI, GitHub Actions, and GitLab CI automate the build, test, and deployment processes, ensuring seamless code integration and deployment with minimal manual intervention.

In essence, crafting a development setup for Flask projects is about judiciously selecting and configuring a suite of tools and practices that collectively foster a productive, seamless, and collaborative development journey. This setup not only streamlines the development process but also ensures the creation of high-quality, maintainable web applications, setting the stage for successful project outcomes.

Chapter One

Getting Started with Flask

Introduction to Flask and its philosophy

Flask emerges as a distinguished micro-framework in the realm of web development, grounded in the Python programming language. Renowned for its straightforwardness and adaptability, Flask has transitioned from its inception as an April Fool's jest into a robust framework adopted by developers globally for a spectrum of web projects, ranging from minimalistic single-page interfaces to elaborate, data-intensive web platforms. This narrative delves into Flask's core ethos, shedding light on the foundational principles and distinctive characteristics that set it apart in the web development sphere.

Central to Flask is an ethos of minimalism paired with the capacity for extensive customization. Flask stands out by providing just the essentials needed for initiating web applications, eschewing the prescriptive nature of more comprehensive frameworks. This 'micro' aspect signifies not a lack of capabilities but a streamlined core that can be expanded through a plethora of extensions, accommodating functionalities such as database integration, form validation, and user authentication, among others.

The guiding philosophy behind Flask advocates for web development to be both straightforward and potent. It builds upon the foundations laid by the Werkzeug WSGI toolkit and the Jinja2 template engine. Werkzeug facilitates the dialog between the web server and the application in adherence to the WSGI standard, ensuring versatility and broad compatibility. Concurrently, Jinja2 offers a dynamic templating language, enabling developers to craft responsive content seamlessly, thus maintaining a clear demarcation between the application logic and its presentation layer.

A pivotal feature of Flask is its intuitive routing system, which adeptly associates URLs with Python-defined "view functions." This system simplifies the creation of RESTful URLs, significantly enhancing the manageability and scalability of web applications. Flask's routing mechanism is designed to support variable rules, handle diverse HTTP methods, and facilitate URL construction, embodying both simplicity and functionality.

Integral to Flask's design philosophy are its built-in development server and interactive debugger. These tools exemplify Flask's commitment to fostering a developer-centric environment, with the server offering a straightforward mechanism for local application testing and the debugger providing detailed error insights to expedite issue resolution. Such features underscore Flask's dedication to streamlining the development process and elevating code quality.

Flask also places a strong emphasis on testing, promoting a test-driven development (TDD) methodology. It includes a test client that mimics application requests and captures the responses, enabling comprehensive unit and functional testing to ensure application robustness and dependability.

The vibrant ecosystem surrounding Flask further embodies its core philosophy. A wide array of extensions enables developers to incorporate various functionalities as needed, advocating for a modular development approach. This ensures that applications remain lightweight and manageable over time.

The extensive documentation and active community support surrounding Flask mirror its guiding principles. Accessible and well-organized documentation caters to developers across the experience spectrum, while the dynamic community offers a rich repository of resources, including tutorials, guides, and extensions, fostering a collaborative and knowledge-sharing culture.

When juxtaposed with other web frameworks, Flask distinguishes itself through its emphasis on simplicity, adaptability, and a non-prescriptive development approach. It contrasts with more structured frameworks by allowing developers to start with a minimal base and scale according to project demands, making Flask suitable for a diverse array of web development projects, from rapid prototyping to complex, large-scale applications.

In essence, Flask's philosophy champions simplicity, adaptability, and expandability. Its lean core, complemented by an extensive ecosystem, presents a balanced web development approach, empowering developers to tailor applications to specific requirements. Flask's straightforward routing, comprehensive development tools, and robust testing support underscore its commitment to a developer-friendly ecosystem. As the web development landscape evolves, Flask's foundational principles ensure its continued relevance and value as a versatile and cherished tool in the developer's arsenal, adept at addressing the multifaceted challenges of contemporary web application development.

Installing Flask and setting up a basic application

Embarking on the journey of installing Flask and crafting a rudimentary web application marks the initial foray into utilizing this highly regarded micro-framework for web development endeavors. Flask, celebrated for its minimalist yet potent framework, offers an ideal platform for developers at various skill levels to create web applications spanning from simple to complex functionalities. This narrative provides a comprehensive walkthrough of the process to install Flask and establish a basic application, simplifying the onset of web development ventures with Flask.

Initial Requirements

The foundational step prior to Flask installation involves ensuring the availability of Python on the system, given Flask's development in the Python environment. Python's appeal lies in its straightforward syntax and extensive support libraries, positioning it as a preferred language for web development tasks. Additionally, the presence of `pip`, Python's package manager, is crucial for installing Python packages, including Flask.

Flask Installation Process

Installing Flask is remarkably uncomplicated, courtesy of `pip`. By executing the command `pip install Flask` within the terminal or command prompt, Flask, along with its dependencies, is seamlessly installed. This ease of installation reflects Flask's philosophy of making web development accessible and streamlined.

Initiating a Basic Flask Application

Following Flask's installation, the subsequent step is to kickstart a basic web application. This involves the creation of a Python script, typically named `**app.py**`, which acts as the application's gateway. Flask's allure is partially attributed to the minimal code required to launch a basic application, underscoring its user-friendly nature.

The inception of `**app.py**` includes importing the Flask class from the Flask package via `**from flask import Flask**`. An instance of this class is then instantiated, conventionally termed `**app: app = Flask(__name__)**`. The usage of `**__name__**` in Flask is pivotal for defining the application's root path, facilitating Flask's resource location capabilities.

Route and View Function Definitions

At the crux of a Flask application are its routes and corresponding view functions. Flask employs the `@app.route` decorator to denote routes, coupled with functions that dictate the content rendered on the webpage. For an elementary application displaying "Hello, World!", a route for the homepage (/) can be established, returning the desired string:

```
@app.route('/')
def hello_world():
    return 'Hello, World!'
```

This `hello_world` function exemplifies a view function, activated when navigating to the application's base URL. Flask's approach to route and view function setup exemplifies its guiding principle of simplicity and adaptability.

Launching the Flask Application

To activate the Flask application, it is requisite to set the Flask environment variable `FLASK_APP` to the newly created Python script `(app.py)`. This is accomplished via terminal commands, `export FLASK_APP=app.py` for Unix/macOS or set `FLASK_APP=app.py` for Windows, followed by initiating the Flask development server with `flask run`. This action spins up a local server, generally accessible at `http://127.0.0.1:5000/`, allowing for browser interactions with the application.

It is imperative to note that the Flask development server is tailored for development purposes, offering features like hot reloading and an interactive debugger. For production environments, a more robust server setup is recommended.

In Summary

The installation of Flask and the configuration of a straightforward web application highlight Flask's dedication to fostering a user-friendly and efficient development environment. These preliminary steps equip developers with the necessary foundation to delve into web development with Flask, characterized by its effortless approach to application setup, route, and view function definition, and development server activation. Flask's streamlined methodology offers a welcoming introduction to the realm of web development, rendering it an appealing option for developers embarking on web projects of varying complexities.

Exploring the Flask application structure

Delving into the architectural design of Flask applications is essential for developers embarking on the creation of web solutions that span a spectrum from straightforward to intricate. Flask's hallmark lies in its uncluttered and flexible nature, attributes that have propelled it to become a preferred framework for web development endeavors. This discourse aims to unravel the intricacies of an optimal organizational framework for Flask applications, underscoring the crucial elements and strategies that underpin the development of effective, scalable, and maintainable web solutions.

Flask Application Architecture Essentials

A Flask application can initially be encapsulated within a single Python script, commonly `app.py`, which encompasses the route definitions, view functions, and the Flask application instance. While this straightforward setup is apt for smaller-scale projects or initial prototypes, it may become unwieldy as the application's complexity escalates, prompting a shift towards a more structured organization.

Refined Flask Application Structure

For more comprehensive applications, a partitioned structure is advocated, segregating the application into distinct sectors, each dedicated to a specific purpose. This segmentation not only enhances code legibility but also simplifies ongoing maintenance efforts. A structured Flask application typically comprises several key components:

- Application Factory: At the forefront of this structured approach is the application factory function, typically situated in `__init__.py` within the application's package. This pivotal function is tasked with generating and configuring the Flask app instance, adaptable to varying configurations suitable for development, testing, and production stages.

- Blueprints: Utilizing Flask Blueprints allows for the compartmentalization of the application into discrete segments, each endowed with its unique routes, templates, and static files. This modularity facilitates the independent development and amalgamation of application features, streamlining the overall development process.

- Data Models: In scenarios involving database interactions, a `models.py` file or a dedicated module is employed to articulate SQLAlchemy models, delineating database schemas and operations. This modular approach aligns with the Model-View-Controller (MVC) architectural paradigm, ensuring a distinct separation of concerns.

- Templates and Static Resources: Flask conventionally manages files from the `templates` and `static` directories for HTML templates and static content such as CSS and JavaScript, respectively. Methodically organizing these files within their respective directories contributes to a coherent and orderly application architecture.

- Form Handling: In instances where web forms are integral, `a **forms.py**` file can centralize form definitions, leveraging extensions like Flask-WTF for efficient form management and validation.

- Configuration Handling: Dedicated configuration files or modules, like `**config.py**`, aggregate all application settings, encompassing database URIs, secret keys, and other configuration parameters, fostering a secure and manageable setup.

- Testing Infrastructure: A specialized testing directory, usually named `**tests**`, accommodates the application's testing framework, advocating for a test-driven development (TDD) methodology to guarantee application integrity and reliability.

Advanced Structural Considerations

For exceptionally intricate applications, additional levels of modularization may be warranted. This might involve breaking down the application into numerous Blueprints, each representing a distinct feature set, and employing an application factory pattern for enhanced configurability and initialization tailored to various scenarios.

- Instance Folder Utilization: Flask advocates for an instance folder, positioned outside the main application package, to store environment-specific configurations and sensitive information, thereby enhancing security by isolating sensitive data from version control systems.

- Utility and Service Layers: For larger applications, dedicated modules for utilities, helper functions, and business logic services abstract common functionalities, reducing complexity and fostering code reuse.

- API Layer Organization: Applications that encompass API functionalities can benefit from a dedicated API module or Blueprint to consolidate API routes, handlers, and response mechanisms, thereby clearly demarcating the API layer from the primary web interface.

- Extension Management: Proper initialization of Flask extensions, such as SQLAlchemy or Flask-Mail, in a distinct module or within the application factory, centralizes extension configurations and simplifies their management.

Adherence to Best Practices

Committing to best practices in the structuring of Flask applications not only smoothens the development journey but also bolsters team collaboration. Thorough documentation, uniform naming conventions, and consistent coding standards render the application architecture intuitive and easily navigable for all team members. The integration of version control systems and the establishment of CI/CD pipelines further underscore a professional and streamlined development regimen.

Synopsis

Mastering the structural nuances of Flask application development is paramount in addressing the growing complexities of web projects. By embracing a well-organized approach, capitalizing on Flask's functionalities such as Blueprints and the application factory concept, and adhering to industry-standard practices, developers are poised to engineer web applications that are not only scalable and maintainable but also conducive to collaborative development efforts. This organized methodology not only eases the development trajectory but also lays a solid groundwork for future enhancements, ensuring the sustained viability of Flask-based initiatives.

Chapter Two

Routing and Views

Understanding URL routing in Flask

Mastering URL routing within the Flask framework is a critical aspect of developing web applications, as it dictates how the application responds to client requests for specific paths. This routing mechanism is a cornerstone of Flask, empowering developers to craft clear and accessible URL patterns that direct users to the appropriate sections of the application. This exploration aims to shed light on the intricacies of URL routing in Flask, detailing its operational framework, adaptability, and the strategies for optimizing its deployment.

Core Principles of URL Routing in Flask

At its essence, URL routing in Flask involves associating view functions with specific URL patterns through decorators, thereby orchestrating the application's response to various client requests. This direct mapping of URLs to Python functions within Flask is what enables the dynamic rendering of content based on the requested URL.

Route Declaration

In Flask, routes are established by employing the `@app.route()` decorator above a view function, with the URL pattern specified as its parameter. This approach to defining routes reflects Flask's commitment to simplicity. A straightforward route definition might appear as follows:

```
@app.route('/')
def homepage():
    return 'Greetings from the Flask App!'
```

Here, the route associated with the application's root ('/') directs requests to the `homepage` view function, which returns a greeting message.

Dynamic Routes

Flask's capability to support dynamic routes, where variables can be integrated into URL paths, enhances the framework's versatility. These variables, encapsulated within `<variable_name>` brackets, are passed as arguments to the view function from the URL, enabling dynamic responses based on the URL path:

```
@app.route('/profile/<user_id>')
def display_profile(user_id):
    return f'Profile for User {user_id}'
```

This example demonstrates a dynamic route that captures a user ID and utilizes it within the `display_profile` function to tailor the response.

Handling HTTP Methods

Routes in Flask can be configured to cater to different HTTP methods, such as GET and POST, by specifying the `methods` parameter in the `@app.route()` decorator. This functionality is essential for creating RESTful APIs, where the request method dictates the action to be executed:

```python
@app.route('/submit', methods=['POST'])
def submit_form():
    # Logic to handle form submission
    pass
```

In this case, the `/submit` route is designed to handle POST requests, typically associated with form submissions.

URL Generation

Flask offers the `url_for()` function for generating URLs to specific functions, enhancing the maintainability of URL structures within the application. By passing the endpoint name and any required arguments to `url_for()`, the function dynamically constructs the appropriate URL, adhering to DRY principles:

```python
from flask import url_for

url_for('display_profile', user_id='123')
```

This usage of `url_for()` dynamically generates the URL for the `display_profile` function with the specified user ID.

Optimizing URL Routing

Implementing best practices in URL routing enhances the clarity and efficiency of Flask applications. Intuitive and descriptive URL patterns not only improve user navigation but also benefit SEO. Thoughtful application of dynamic routing ensures flexibility, while consistent URL structures and naming conventions contribute to a cohesive application architecture. Utilizing `url_for()` for internal URL generation promotes decoupling and adaptability in the routing system.

Synopsis

Grasping the nuances of URL routing is fundamental to crafting web applications with Flask, as it shapes the application's interaction with user requests. Flask's routing architecture provides a balance of straightforwardness and capability, enabling the definition of expressive URL patterns essential for the application's functionality. By embracing Flask's routing paradigms and adhering to best practices, developers can create applications that are not only functional but also intuitive and poised for growth, delivering a seamless user experience and accommodating future expansions.

Building views and handling HTTP methods

Crafting views and adeptly handling HTTP methods within the Flask framework are crucial for orchestrating how web applications process user inquiries and return specific outcomes. In Flask, views are essentially Python functions that take requests and produce HTTP responses, playing a key role in the application's interactive elements. Moreover, the nuanced management of HTTP methods such as GET, POST, PUT, and DELETE within these views is vital for fostering dynamic and engaging web environments. This narrative aims to dissect the methodologies behind constructing views in Flask, the intricacies involved in handling HTTP methods, and the recommended approaches for refining these processes.

Crafting Views in Flask

In the Flask environment, views are delineated as functions that issue HTTP responses to incoming requests, thereby directing the application's response mechanisms. Establishing a view involves utilizing the `@app.route()` decorator to associate a Python function with a specific URL route, creating a conduit for processing requests. For instance, a simple view definition might be structured as follows:

```
@app.route('/welcome')
def welcome():
    return 'Hello from our Flask Application!'
```

Here, the `welcome` function is linked to the `/welcome` URL, and accessing this URL triggers the function to respond with a greeting, illustrating the foundational operation of view functions in Flask.

Management of HTTP Methods

HTTP methods delineate the intended action for a resource within a web request, forming the backbone of interaction within web applications. Flask's view functions can be tailored to handle various HTTP methods by specifying them in the `methods` parameter of the `@app.route()` decorator. The essential HTTP methods encompass:

- **GET**: Primarily used to retrieve data from a resource, typical for page requests.

- **POST**: Utilized for submitting data to a resource for processing, often associated with form submissions.

- **PUT**: Applied to update or replace a resource's existing data.

- **DELETE**: Used to eliminate the specified resource.

A representative Flask view that accommodates both GET and POST requests could be depicted as:

```python
@app.route('/process', methods=['GET', 'POST'])
def process():
    if request.method == 'POST':
        # Execute form processing
        return redirect(url_for('main'))
    return render_template('submission.html')
```

In this scenario, the **process** view handles GET requests by displaying a submission form and processes submitted data on POST requests, subsequently redirecting to the main page.

Optimizing View Construction and HTTP Method Handling

Employing best practices in the formulation of views and the management of HTTP methods can significantly enhance the Flask application's development, scalability, and maintenance. Key practices include:

- Blueprints for Organization: Segmenting views into Blueprints facilitates modular development, particularly for expansive applications, aiding in organization and scalability.

- Validation of Inputs: Essential for views processing POST requests to ensure the integrity and security of incoming data.

- DRY Principle Adherence: Reducing code redundancy by leveraging utility functions for common operations across multiple views.

- Method Specification: Defining the permitted HTTP methods for each view to ensure precise and efficient request handling.

- Robust Error Management: Incorporating comprehensive error handling within views to address exceptions effectively and provide clear feedback.

Synopsis

The development of views and the proficient management of HTTP methods are foundational to the operability of Flask-based web applications. By engineering views that adeptly cater to a variety of HTTP requests, developers can create web applications that are both interactive and user-friendly. Implementing best practices in the design of these views and the handling of HTTP methods not only streamlines the development process but also fortifies the application's security, efficiency, and capacity for growth. With a thorough grasp of these principles, developers can exploit Flask's full potential to construct sophisticated web applications that adeptly meet contemporary web engagement standards.

Using dynamic route parameters

Incorporating dynamic route parameters within Flask enhances the adaptability and user engagement of web applications by enabling URLs to capture variable data directly. This functionality facilitates the crafting of responsive and tailored web experiences, allowing applications to serve customized content based on user-driven URL paths. This discussion delves into the essence of dynamic route parameters in Flask, detailing their operational mechanics, advantages, and the recommended approaches for their optimal utilization.

Dynamic Route Parameters Explained

Dynamic route parameters are variable segments within a Flask route's URL pattern, designated by angle brackets `< >` that encapsulate the variable name. These parameters dynamically adjust based on the URL accessed, with Flask automatically extracting these values and passing them to the corresponding view function as arguments.

Deploying Dynamic Routes

To deploy dynamic routes in Flask, developers define routes with variable sections embedded within the URL pattern. An illustrative example is as follows:

```python
@app.route('/article/<int:article_id>')
def display_article(article_id):
    # Logic to fetch and render the article by article_id
    return f'Article {article_id}'
```

Here, the route `/article/<int:article_id>` features a dynamic parameter **`article_id`** that anticipates an integer value. The **`display_article`** function then receives this value, enabling specific operations tailored to the requested article ID.

Varieties of Dynamic Parameters

Flask supports multiple types of dynamic parameters by specifying a converter type within the route definition. Notable converter types include:

- **string**: Captures any text except slashes, used by default when no converter is specified.

- **int**: Accepts positive integer values.

- **float**: Allows for positive floating-point numbers.

- **path**: Similar to `string` but includes slashes.

- **uuid**: Accepts strings formatted as UUIDs.

Selecting an appropriate converter type ensures that dynamic parameters conform to the intended format, facilitating efficient URL parsing.

Advantages of Employing Dynamic Route Parameters

The use of dynamic route parameters in web development brings several key benefits:

- Adaptability: They enable URLs to flexibly cater to diverse content or actions, enhancing the application's versatility.

- Scalability: With dynamic parameters, applications can easily expand, accommodating new content or features without restructuring the URL schema.

- Streamlined URLs: They contribute to the creation of more concise and meaningful URLs, elevating the user experience and potentially improving search engine rankings.

- Operational Efficiency: Capturing variable data from the URL streamlines the request handling process, eliminating the need for additional query parameters or path adjustments.

Best Practices in Leveraging Dynamic Route Parameters

For the effective application of dynamic route parameters in Flask, certain best practices are recommended:

- Clarity in Parameter Naming: Employ descriptive and intuitive names for dynamic parameters to enhance the readability and maintainability of the code.

- Judicious Converter Type Selection: Opt for the most fitting converter type for each dynamic parameter to ensure accurate validation and streamlined error handling.

- Simplicity in Route Design: Although dynamic parameters provide significant flexibility, overly intricate routes can become cumbersome to manage. Aim for straightforward and clear route configurations.

- Robust Error Management: Within view functions, robust error handling mechanisms should be in place to gracefully address scenarios where dynamic parameters do not align with expected formats or refer to invalid resources.

Synopsis

Dynamic route parameters stand as a significant feature in Flask, enabling developers to build web applications that respond dynamically to user interactions through URL paths. By mastering the implementation and management of these parameters, developers can harness Flask's routing capabilities to deliver web experiences that are both personalized and interactive. Following established best practices in the use of dynamic route parameters ensures that applications are scalable, easily maintained, and intuitive, thereby enriching the overall user experience and facilitating the sustained success of the web application.

Chapter Three

Templates and Static Files

Introduction to Jinja2 templating

Jinja2 emerges as a cornerstone templating engine within the Python landscape, notably for its seamless melding with the Flask framework, streamlining the crafting of dynamic web pages by marrying data with HTML templates. This primer delves into the foundational aspects of Jinja2, highlighting its essential features, the syntax it employs, and the array of advantages it offers to the realm of web development, coupled with recommended practices for its adept application.

Fundamentals of Jinja2 Templating

Jinja2's design ethos is centered around enhancing web development efficiency, allowing for the integration of Python-esque expressions within HTML to facilitate the dynamic rendering of content. This delineation of logic from presentation adheres to contemporary web design principles, ensuring applications remain both scalable and maintainable.

Key Features of Jinja2

The Jinja2 templating engine is renowned for its comprehensive feature set, which includes:

- Dynamic Content Insertion: Variables from Flask view functions can be seamlessly integrated into the HTML, enabling the real-time rendering of content.

- Control Statements: Jinja2 templates can incorporate loops and conditional statements, allowing for sophisticated data presentation directly within the template.

- Template Inheritance: This feature allows the definition of a base template that outlines a general layout, which can be extended or overridden by child templates, promoting reuse and consistency.

- Data Transformation and Formatting: Through a variety of available filters and tests, variables can be formatted or transformed before being displayed, enhancing template versatility.

Syntax Overview

Jinja2's syntax is intentionally designed to be intuitive for those with Python experience, with key elements including:

- **Variable Markers**: Enclosed within `{{ }}`, these markers denote where variables will be substituted within the template.

- **Control Statements**: Wrapped in `{% %}`, these denote control structures like loops and conditional blocks within the template.

- **Template Comments**: Designated by `{# #}`, these allow for non-rendering annotations within the template for developer clarity.

Flask Integration

The integration of Jinja2 with Flask is designed to be straightforward, with Flask's `render_template` function processing templates through Jinja2, binding data to templates before serving the resultant HTML.

Benefits Brought by Jinja2

Jinja2 templating introduces several benefits to web development, including:

- Development Efficiency: The clear separation of HTML and Python logic facilitated by Jinja2 leads to more maintainable codebases.

- Content Presentation Flexibility: Jinja2's support for in-template logic and inheritance grants developers significant control over how content is displayed.

- Optimized Performance: Jinja2 is engineered for speed, ensuring that template rendering does not become a bottleneck.

Jinja2 Templating Best Practices

Effective utilization of Jinja2 involves a set of best practices, such as:

- Minimizing In-Template Logic: Keeping logic within templates to a minimum and relegating business logic to the view functions can greatly enhance code readability and maintainability.

- Adhering to a Consistent Template Structure: Using template inheritance and maintaining a consistent structure across templates simplifies management and ensures uniformity.

- Safe Variable Rendering: Given potential security risks like XSS, careful handling of variable rendering is advised, with Jinja2's auto-escaping feature offering an added layer of security.

Conclusion

Jinja2 stands as an indispensable templating engine in the Flask ecosystem, empowering developers to construct dynamic, data-driven web interfaces with heightened efficiency and adaptability. Grasping the fundamentals of Jinja2, along with its syntax and integration with Flask, and adhering to established best practices, enables developers to fully leverage Jinja2's capabilities, paving the way for the development of sophisticated and maintainable web applications. Jinja2's contribution to the web development process underscores its value as a crucial tool in the web developer's arsenal, facilitating the creation of engaging and interactive web experiences.

Rendering templates and passing data to them

In the realm of Flask-powered web application creation, the art of blending HTML templates with live data stands as a critical practice, enabling the dynamic evolution of web page content in response to user actions or changes in the application's state. This process, central to the Flask framework, involves the integration of variable data within

HTML templates to produce web pages that can adapt and respond in real-time. This discourse seeks to shed light on the intricacies of template rendering within Flask, the approach to infusing templates with dynamic data, and the guiding principles to optimize this practice for enhanced application performance and maintainability.

Rendering Templates in Flask

At the core of Flask's functionality is its use of the Jinja2 templating engine, renowned for its ability to interweave Pythonic data constructs within HTML, facilitating the real-time rendering of web content. The act of rendering a template is accomplished through Flask's `render_template()` function, which requires the designation of the template file and any associated key-value pairs representing the dynamic content to be incorporated. For instance:

```python
from flask import render_template

@app.route('/dashboard/<user>')
def dashboard(user):
    return render_template('dashboard.html', username=user)
```

Here, the `render_template()` function is tasked with rendering the `dashboard.html` template, dynamically populating the **username** variable within the template with the value obtained from the `user` parameter in the URL.

Data Infusion into Templates

The mechanism for transmitting data to Jinja2 templates in Flask is facilitated by the versatile `render_template()` function, capable of handling an array of keyword arguments that map directly to the template's variables. This allows for the transmission of data ranging from simple strings to complex data structures, enabling intricate data manipulation and presentation within the template.

Context Variables in Templates

Flask inherently provides a suite of context variables that are automatically accessible within templates, such as `request`, `session`, and `g`. These variables offer a gateway to request-specific data, session-related information, and global application data, respectively, further empowering templates to dynamically reflect the nuances of the application's context or user-specific data.

Enhancing Template Rendering and Data Infusion Practices

To ensure the process of rendering templates and infusing them with data remains streamlined and effective, adherence to a set of best practices is recommended:

- Distinction Between Logic and Presentation: It is advisable to confine business logic to view functions or models, reserving templates primarily for rendering purposes to maintain a clean separation of concerns.

- Restrained Use of Logic in Templates: While Jinja2 templates support logical constructs like loops and conditional statements, maintaining a minimalistic approach to logic within templates is key to preserving their clarity.

- Uniform and Descriptive Variable Naming: Employing consistent and descriptive naming for variables passed to templates aids in enhancing code readability and reducing potential ambiguities.

- Strategic Use of Template Inheritance: Leveraging the template inheritance feature in Jinja2 to define a base template that establishes a common structure for child templates promotes consistency and reusability across the application.

- Attention to Security Measures: Given the potential security implications, especially when rendering user-generated content, it is crucial to utilize Jinja2's auto-escaping feature to mitigate risks such as Cross-Site Scripting (XSS) attacks, ensuring data is appropriately sanitized.

Conclusion

The technique of rendering templates and embedding them with dynamic data is a cornerstone of building Flask-based web applications, enabling the creation of web pages that dynamically adapt to user interactions and application states. By delving into the functionality of the Jinja2 templating engine, adeptly incorporating data into templates, and following established best practices, developers can forge web applications that are not only dynamic and engaging but also secure, maintainable, and poised for scalability. Through meticulous template rendering and data infusion, Flask applications can deliver rich, customized web experiences, catering effectively to the evolving demands of modern web users.

Organizing and serving static files

In the landscape of web application development with Flask, effectively managing and deploying static assets such as CSS files, JavaScript, and images is crucial for enhancing user engagement and optimizing application performance. Flask, renowned for its simplicity and efficiency, provides a straightforward methodology for handling these resources, ensuring they are well-organized and accessible. This discourse delves into the strategies for structuring and delivering static files in Flask, underscoring the framework's inherent features, recommended organizational tactics for static content, and methods to refine their delivery.

Flask's Strategy for Static Assets

Flask inherently earmarks a directory named `static` located at the application's root level to store static resources. This setup allows for an intuitive management system for these files, enabling straightforward referencing within the application. The handling of requests to the `/static` endpoint is seamlessly managed by the web server when Flask applications are operational, directing the server to fetch the appropriate files from the `static` directory.

Structuring Static Assets

While a singular `static` directory may suffice for smaller applications, a more nuanced structure becomes imperative as the application's complexity escalates. It is advisable to categorize static assets into subdirectories, such as `css`, `js`, and `images`, within the `static` folder to enhance navigability and management. An example structure could be:

```
/static
    /css
        main.css
    /js
        script.js
    /images
        header.png
```

This organized approach facilitates the segregation of various asset types, streamlining

the maintenance of the application's static resources.

Delivering Static Files in Flask

To reference static assets within HTML templates, Flask employs the `url_for` function with the **'static'** endpoint, ensuring the generation of accurate file paths. For instance, embedding a CSS file within an HTML template can be achieved as follows:

```
<link rel="stylesheet" href="{{ url_for('static', filename='css/main.css') }}">
```

This technique guarantees the dynamic generation of the correct path to the static asset, accommodating the application's configuration and URL structure.

Recommended Practices for Managing Static Assets

To optimize the handling of static files in Flask applications, adherence to certain best practices is recommended:

- Implementing Asset Versioning: Utilizing a versioning scheme for static files can aid in circumventing caching issues, ensuring users access the most current versions.

- Asset Minification and Concatenation: Minimizing file sizes and consolidating multiple files can significantly enhance loading times and reduce server requests.

- Leveraging CDNs: For applications experiencing substantial traffic, deploying static files via a CDN can diminish latency, improve load times, and alleviate bandwidth demands on the primary server.

- Ensuring Secure Delivery: It is essential to verify that static files are devoid of sensitive data and are transmitted securely over HTTPS.

Enhancing the Efficiency of Static File Delivery

Further optimizations in the delivery of static assets can be achieved through:

- Configuring HTTP Caching: Setting appropriate cache headers for static assets can exploit browser caching, minimizing server load and enhancing client-side performance.

- Employing Compression: Compressing static files, such as through Gzip, can reduce their size, accelerating network transfer speeds.

- Asynchronous JavaScript Loading: Opting for asynchronous or deferred loading of JavaScript files can improve page rendering times by preventing the blocking of other page elements.

Conclusion

The adept organization and provisioning of static files are integral to the efficacy and user experience of Flask-powered web applications. By embracing Flask's conventional methodologies, implementing a structured approach to static asset organization, and adhering to best practices for asset delivery, developers can ensure efficient and secure access to static resources. Through meticulous management and strategic optimization of static asset delivery, Flask applications can attain enhanced performance, scalability, and maintainability, contributing to a fluid and compelling user experience.

Chapter Four

Forms and User Input

Handling form submissions with Flask-WTF

Managing form submissions within Flask-based web applications is a fundamental aspect that entails gathering user inputs securely and effectively. The Flask-WTF extension enriches this process by offering a streamlined framework for form construction, validation, and processing, tailored specifically for Flask environments. This narrative seeks to elucidate the facets of handling form submissions via Flask-WTF, highlighting its integration with Flask, the formulation of form classes, the authentication of form inputs, and the established practices for optimizing the use of this potent extension.

Flask-WTF Overview

Flask-WTF extends the capabilities of WTForms, a comprehensive library for handling forms in Python, by incorporating additional features that facilitate seamless integration with Flask. It simplifies the creation of forms, ensures robust data validation, and fortifies forms against CSRF (Cross-Site Request Forgery) attacks, thereby bolstering the security and functionality of form operations in web applications.

Flask-WTF Integration

To harness Flask-WTF within a Flask application, the extension must first be installed and imported. A crucial step in this integration is the configuration of a secret key for the application, which serves as a safeguard against CSRF threats, a vital security measure for handling form submissions:

```python
from flask import Flask
from flask_wtf import FlaskForm
from wtforms import StringField, SubmitField
from wtforms.validators import DataRequired

app = Flask(__name__)
app.config['SECRET_KEY'] = 'your_secure_key'
```

Constructing Form Classes via Flask-WTF

With Flask-WTF, form structures are defined using classes, where each form field, such as **`StringField`** or **`PasswordField`**, mirrors a distinct HTML form element. Validators are applied to enforce specific rules or conditions on the user-provided data:

```python
class ContactForm(FlaskForm):
    name = StringField('Name', validators=[DataRequired()])
    submit = SubmitField('Send')
```

This example delineates a **`ContactForm`** with a mandatory text field for the user's name and a submission button.

Form Rendering in Jinja2 Templates

Flask-WTF enables the straightforward rendering of forms within Jinja2 templates. The form fields are accessible as attributes of the form instance passed to the template, with Flask-WTF offering methods for rendering fields, labels, and validation messages:

```html
<form method="post">
    {{ form.hidden_tag() }}
    {{ form.name.label }} {{ form.name() }}
    {{ form.submit() }}
</form>
```

The inclusion of `**hidden_tag()**` is essential for rendering hidden fields, including the CSRF token, crucial for CSRF defense.

Authenticating and Processing Form Inputs

Flask-WTF streamlines the validation of submitted form data against predefined constraints using the `**validate_on_submit()**` method, which activates the validators associated with each field upon form submission:

```python
@app.route('/feedback', methods=['GET', 'POST'])
def feedback():
    form = ContactForm()
    if form.validate_on_submit():
        # Handle validated form data
        return redirect(url_for('thank_you'))
    return render_template('feedback.html', form=form)
```

This structure efficiently manages form submissions, differentiating between displaying the form and processing validated inputs.

Flask-WTF Form Handling Best Practices

To fully leverage Flask-WTF's form handling capabilities, adherence to several best practices is recommended:

- Ensuring CSRF Protection: The `form.hidden_tag()` should always be included in the form template to embed the CSRF token field, fortifying the form against CSRF exploits.

- Providing Validation Feedback: Flask-WTF supports inline validation feedback in templates, enabling immediate and clear communication of errors to users.

- Customizing Field Widgets: Flask-WTF's compatibility with custom field widgets and styles allows for enhanced form aesthetics and user interaction.

- Securing Form Data: It's imperative to process form data securely, especially when dealing with sensitive information, and to consider additional precautions such as input sanitization and output escaping.

Conclusion

Navigating form submissions with Flask-WTF presents a robust, secure methodology for managing user inputs in Flask web applications. By adhering to the conventions set forth by Flask-WTF for constructing, validating, and rendering forms, developers can implement form handling mechanisms that are both efficient and user-centric. Embracing established best practices for form security, user feedback, and interface customization further elevates the efficacy and security of web forms, contributing to the overall integrity and user experience of the application. Flask-WTF thus simplifies the complexities associated with form handling, allowing developers to concentrate on crafting feature-rich and secure web applications.

Form validation and error handling

In the sphere of web application creation, especially within Flask environments, the tasks of validating forms and managing errors are crucial for maintaining data accuracy and enhancing user interactions. These processes ensure that user-provided information meets specific standards before being accepted, thus protecting the application from incorrect or potentially harmful inputs. Additionally, proficient error management improves the interaction experience by offering users detailed feedback on any issues encountered during form submissions. This essay aims to delve into the intricacies of form validation and error management, underlining their significance, implementation techniques, and the guidelines for their optimal application in the context of web development.

Importance of Form Validation

The primary goal of form validation is to act as a guardian, confirming that incoming data aligns with set requirements. This involves checking that user entries are complete, accurate, and formatted correctly, thereby ensuring the reliability and uniformity of the data. Key advantages of stringent form validation encompass:

- Maintaining Data Quality: Through validation, the accuracy and completeness of user inputs are verified, preserving the data's integrity.

- Bolstering Security Measures: Validation aids in mitigating prevalent security risks such as injection flaws, thereby safeguarding the application.

- Enhancing the User Journey: By providing immediate feedback, validation facilitates error correction by users, streamlining the submission process.

Form Validation Techniques

Form validation can be approached in several ways, notably:

- Validation on the Client Side: Carried out within the browser using JavaScript, this validation type offers quick feedback, helping reduce server workload by catching typical input errors upfront.

- Validation on the Server Side: Performed after the form has been submitted to the server, this layer of validation is essential for ensuring the overall security and integrity of the data, serving as a definitive check before any data processing.

A comprehensive validation strategy usually combines both client-side and server-side validation, striking a balance between user experience and data security.

Strategies for Error Handling in Form Submissions

Error handling, in the context of form submissions, revolves around identifying validation failures and other issues, then clearly communicating these to the user. Effective error handling strategies involve:

- Providing Detailed Error Messages: Offering specific, actionable feedback for each error helps users understand and rectify their mistakes.

- Emphasizing Fields with Errors: Using visual cues to highlight erroneous fields draws user attention to the areas needing correction.

- Retaining User Entries: Keeping previously entered information (except sensitive fields) when re-displaying a form for corrections prevents user frustration and data loss.

Best Practices for Form Validation and Error Handling

To maximize the efficiency of form validation and error handling, several best practices are recommended:

- Validate Early and Validate Often: Implementing validation at multiple points, from initial client-side checks to comprehensive server-side validation, enhances both security and user experience.

- Adopt a Conservative Approach: Accept only the necessary input for the application's functionality, rejecting all other data by default.

- Leverage Existing Tools: Utilizing well-established validation libraries and frameworks can streamline development, providing ready-made rules for validation and error handling.

- Keep Validation Rules Current: Regular updates to validation rules and error messages are crucial to keeping pace with changing application needs and emerging security concerns.

- Thoroughly Test Validation Mechanisms: Rigorous testing of validation and error handling ensures their reliability across various scenarios, including edge cases and security tests.

Conclusion

Validation of forms and management of errors are fundamental to constructing secure, accurate, and user-friendly web applications. By implementing comprehensive validation checks and offering detailed, constructive error feedback, developers not only ensure the integrity of data and protect against vulnerabilities but also foster a positive user experience. Committing to the continuous refinement of validation and error handling practices, in line with evolving application requirements and security standards, is key to developing robust, engaging web platforms. Through diligent adherence to these principles, developers are equipped to create web environments that are both secure and inviting for user interaction.

CSRF protection

In the sphere of securing web applications, Cross-Site Request Forgery (CSRF) protection emerges as a critical layer of defense. CSRF vulnerabilities exploit the trust a web application places in an authenticated user's browser, enabling attackers to carry out unauthorized actions under the guise of the user. Establishing solid CSRF safeguarding protocols is vital to preserving the sanctity and security of user transactions and engagements within web applications.

Exploring CSRF Vulnerabilities

CSRF attacks manipulate users into inadvertently executing actions within a web application where they're authenticated, often through deceptive links or embedded malicious scripts on third-party sites. Such exploitations can lead to unauthorized modifications or data breaches, compromising user and application security.

Foundations of CSRF Protection

At the heart of thwarting CSRF threats lies the implementation of anti-CSRF tokens—distinct, unpredictable sequences of characters linked to the user's session. These tokens are incorporated within web forms and undergo scrutiny on the server upon the form's submission. The underlying principle is that while an attacker might forge a request, duplicating a valid, session-bound token is significantly more arduous.

Instituting CSRF Safeguards

1. Crafting Tokens: Distinct tokens should be generated for each user session and discreetly incorporated within

forms, serving as cryptographic nonces to guarantee the uniqueness of each submission.

2. Assessing Tokens: Server-side validation of the CSRF token against the session-stored token is crucial when a form is submitted. Any inconsistency or absence of the token should lead to the invalidation of the request.

3. Refreshing Tokens: Refreshing CSRF tokens at regular intervals and after significant session events, such as user logins, helps mitigate potential token theft risks.

Optimal CSRF Defense Practices

- Leveraging Framework Capabilities: Many web development frameworks, including Flask and Django, come equipped with CSRF protection features. Utilizing these built-in mechanisms can simplify the establishment of CSRF defenses.

- Maintaining Token Security: CSRF tokens should be handled with the utmost security, ensuring they're transmitted securely, not exposed in URLs, and shielded from referrer header leaks.

- Adopting the Double Submit Cookie Strategy: This approach involves validating the CSRF token in the form against a token stored in a cookie, adding an extra layer of defense by exploiting the browser's restriction on setting custom headers for cross-origin requests.

- Utilizing Custom Headers for AJAX: Embedding CSRF tokens within custom headers for AJAX requests bolsters security, as such headers can't be appended to cross-site requests by browsers.

Advancements in CSRF Defense

The continuous evolution of web technologies and the sophistication of cyber threats necessitate the advancement of CSRF defense mechanisms. Modern strategies must cover traditional form submissions, AJAX interactions, and API communications to ensure comprehensive protection.

Embracing SameSite Cookie Attributes

The advent of the SameSite cookie attribute marks a significant advancement in CSRF protection, directing browsers to only send cookies with requests originating from the same domain. This attribute effectively counters numerous CSRF attack avenues by ensuring that session-related cookies aren't transmitted with requests from external domains.

Conclusion

CSRF protection is an indispensable facet of web application security architecture, safeguarding against unauthorized actions that could endanger user data and the integrity of application functionalities. By deploying token-based CSRF defenses, adhering to secure token management practices, and harnessing the security features offered by development frameworks, developers can shield their applications from CSRF threats. As web technologies progress, CSRF protection strategies must evolve correspondingly to address new vulnerabilities, ensuring the ongoing security and reliability of web applications. Prioritizing CSRF protection not only fortifies the security of web applications but also reinforces user trust in these platforms, protecting personal and application data from unauthorized access and alterations.

Chapter Five

Databases in Flask

Overview of Flask-SQLAlchemy

Flask-SQLAlchemy stands as an integral extension that merges Flask, a popular web framework, with SQLAlchemy, an ORM library, providing a harmonized and Pythonic way to manage database interactions within Flask projects. This extension enriches the robust features of SQLAlchemy by incorporating Flask-specific enhancements that simplify the execution of database tasks and the administration of data models. This overview seeks to illuminate the essence of Flask-SQLAlchemy, delving into its operational advantages and its crucial role in facilitating database-oriented operations in Flask-based projects.

Flask-SQLAlchemy Essentials

Flask-SQLAlchemy acts as a liaison between Flask applications and various database engines, simplifying direct database interactions through ORM techniques. It allows developers to define database schemas as Python classes, which translate to database tables, enabling the manipulation of database entries as Python objects. This layer of abstraction enhances code legibility and maintenance while bolstering security by mitigating SQL injection risks.

Flask-SQLAlchemy's Salient Features

Flask-SQLAlchemy is characterized by its distinctive features that make it a preferred choice among Flask developers:

- Ease of Configuration: Setting up Flask-SQLAlchemy in Flask applications is straightforward, with the extension using Flask's configuration settings to manage database connections and preferences.

- Comprehensive ORM Features: Leveraging SQLAlchemy's capabilities, Flask-SQLAlchemy provides a wide range of ORM functionalities, including support for advanced queries, data relationships, and migrations, making it a versatile tool for database operations.

- Compatibility with Various Databases: Flask-SQLAlchemy's ability to work with multiple database systems, including SQLite, PostgreSQL, and MySQL, offers developers the flexibility to select the most suitable database backend for their projects.

- Seamless Flask Integration: Flask-SQLAlchemy is designed to integrate effortlessly with Flask's architecture and related extensions, such as Flask-Migrate for database migration tasks, ensuring a cohesive development experience.

Deploying Flask-SQLAlchemy in Development

Integrating Flask-SQLAlchemy into a project involves creating models that reflect the structure of database tables, utilizing the `**db.Model**` base class provided by the extension, and defining attributes that correspond to table columns:

```python
from flask_sqlalchemy import SQLAlchemy

db = SQLAlchemy(app)

class Account(db.Model):
    id = db.Column(db.Integer, primary_key=True)
    username = db.Column(db.String(80), unique=True, nullable=False)
    email = db.Column(db.String(120), unique=True, nullable=False)
```

This example demonstrates the establishment of an `Account` model with `id`, `username`, and `email` attributes, mirroring the database table configuration.

Querying and Managing Data

Flask-SQLAlchemy facilitates the querying and management of database records through its ORM interface, enabling the performance of CRUD operations using Python syntax, thus abstracting the complexity of SQL:

```python
# Creating a new account
new_account = Account(username='alex_doe', email='alex@example.com')
db.session.add(new_account)
db.session.commit()

# Fetching accounts
accounts = Account.query.all()

# Updating an account's information
account = Account.query.filter_by(username='alex_doe').first()
account.email = 'alex.doe@example.com'
db.session.commit()

# Removing an account
db.session.delete(account)
db.session.commit()
```

Best Practices with Flask-SQLAlchemy

Following best practices with Flask-SQLAlchemy can significantly enhance its effectiveness:

- Modularizing Model Definitions: Structuring data models in separate modules or packages can aid in the application's scalability and maintainability.

- Query Optimization: Making use of Flask-SQLAlchemy's query capabilities to retrieve only necessary data can optimize database performance and minimize load.

- Diligent Session Management: Proper management of database sessions, ensuring timely commits or rollbacks, is essential for data consistency.

- Prioritizing Security Measures: Paying attention to security, especially concerning user-generated data, is crucial to prevent vulnerabilities such as SQL injection.

Conclusion

Flask-SQLAlchemy serves as an indispensable tool in the Flask ecosystem, streamlining database interactions and data model management through its Pythonic approach. By offering a flexible ORM layer that is agnostic to the underlying database technology, Flask-SQLAlchemy empowers developers to efficiently build data-driven Flask applications. Adopting Flask-SQLAlchemy's functionalities and adhering to established best practices can markedly improve the development process, maintainability, and performance of Flask projects, solidifying its position as a vital asset in Flask application development.

Defining models and creating a database

In the realm of Flask web development, particularly when utilizing extensions like SQLAlchemy or Flask-SQLAlchemy, the establishment of models and the subsequent database creation are pivotal elements that underpin efficient data management. Models act as architectural blueprints for database tables, delineating the data's structure, relationships, and operational logic, thereby forming the cornerstone of data storage and retrieval mechanisms within the application. This narrative seeks to illuminate the methodologies involved in model definition and database instantiation, underscoring their critical role in the developmental lifecycle of Flask-based applications.

Model Definition in Flask

Within the Flask framework, especially with SQLAlchemy or Flask-SQLAlchemy, models are articulated through Python classes. Each class mirrors a database table, with class attributes representing the table's columns. This ORM paradigm facilitates a more natural interaction with the database, employing Pythonic expressions.

A typical model encompasses:

- Column Specifications: Model attributes are specified using SQLAlchemy's column types like `**Integer**`, `**String**`, `**DateTime**`, which define the nature and data type of each database column.

- Identification Keys: Models are expected to have a primary key attribute, serving as a unique identifier for table records.

- Table Relationships: Models may also articulate the interconnections between tables, such as one-to-many or many-to-many relationships, fostering data association across diverse tables.

Illustration of Model Construction

```
from flask_sqlalchemy import SQLAlchemy

db = SQLAlchemy()

class User(db.Model):
    id = db.Column(db.Integer, primary_key=True)
    username = db.Column(db.String(80), unique=True, nullable=False)
    email = db.Column(db.String(120), unique=True, nullable=False)
    posts = db.relationship('Post', backref='author', lazy='dynamic')

class Post(db.Model):
    id = db.Column(db.Integer, primary_key=True)
    title = db.Column(db.String(100), nullable=False)
    body = db.Column(db.Text, nullable=False)
    user_id = db.Column(db.Integer, db.ForeignKey('user.id'), nullable=False)
```

This example delineates the construction of `User` and `Post` models, typical of a blogging platform, where users have multiple associated posts, demonstrating the definition of relationships.

Database Initialization

Following the definition of models, the subsequent phase involves the instantiation of the database and its tables. Flask-SQLAlchemy simplifies this with the `create_all()` method, which inspects the models and erects the requisite database tables based on the defined models.

To instantiate a database:

1. Database URI Configuration: The application must be configured with the database URI, indicating the database type and location.

2. Flask-SQLAlchemy Initialization: The Flask-SQLAlchemy extension should be initialized with the Flask application instance.

3. Execution of create_all(): Employing `db.create_all()` post model definition and application initialization leads to the creation of database tables, contingent upon their non-existence.

Model and Database Creation Best Practices

- Structured Design: Segregating models into distinct modules or files enhances the application's clarity and maintainability as it evolves.

- Upholding Data Integrity: Employing SQLAlchemy's constraints like `nullable=False` or `unique=True` within models ensures the database's data integrity.

- Migration Handling: For applications undergoing schema evolution, migration tools like Flask-Migrate are instrumental in managing schema alterations without data loss.

- Security Measures: It is imperative to handle sensitive data with care, such as encrypting passwords, to preserve the application's security integrity.

Conclusion

The articulation of models and the generation of a database are foundational activities in the Flask application development process, crucial for effective data governance. Through the ORM methodology enabled by SQLAlchemy and Flask-SQLAlchemy, developers can define data architectures and relationships in an intuitive manner, promoting development efficiency and application maintainability. Adherence to established practices in model formulation and database management is essential for ensuring the application's scalability, data integrity, and security. As applications grow and transform, the ability to maintain a resilient and adaptable data model underscores the importance of meticulous model definition and database establishment in the Flask development paradigm.

Performing CRUD operations

Within the sphere of web development, especially when it comes to building database-centric applications, carrying out CRUD (Create, Read, Update, Delete) operations is integral to facilitating vibrant data exchanges. These processes allow an application to interface with its database, enabling the addition of fresh entries, retrieval of stored data, updates to current information, and removal of outdated entries. For developers, grasping the intricacies of CRUD operations is crucial for the effective orchestration of data within their applications, ensuring the data remains current, accessible, and accurate. This discussion aims to delve into the details of executing CRUD operations, shedding light on their critical role and the approaches used in their implementation across web applications.

Core Functions of CRUD Operations

CRUD operations embody the fundamental interactions with database entities, encapsulating the entire range of data engagements within an application:

- Create: This action involves adding new data entries to the database, typically facilitated through user input forms within a web interface.

- Read: This action involves retrieving existing data from the database, enabling its display or usage within the application.

- Update: This action involves altering data that's already present in the database, ensuring the information stays relevant and precise.

- Delete: This action involves erasing data from the database, critical for discarding data that's no longer necessary, thereby enhancing the database's performance.

Implementing CRUD Operations

The execution of CRUD operations may differ based on the chosen tech stack and the specific database system employed. Nonetheless, the underlying principles are consistent across various platforms.

Operation to Create

The process of creating new records generally involves collecting data through user interfaces, verifying this data for accuracy, and then executing a command (like an INSERT statement or ORM method) to add this data to the designated database table.

```python
# Demonstrating a Create operation with SQLAlchemy
new_profile = User(username='alice_doe', email='alice.doe@example.com')
db.session.add(new_profile)
db.session.commit()
```

Operation to Read

Retrieving data is achieved with commands (such as SELECT statements or ORM queries) that define the criteria for the data to be fetched. The data that's fetched can then be displayed to the user or used for additional processing within the application.

```python
# Demonstrating a Read operation with SQLAlchemy
all_profiles = User.query.all()
```

Operation to Update

Updating records involves pinpointing the specific record(s) to be updated, modifying the relevant attributes, and then saving those modifications back to the database using commands (like UPDATE statements or ORM methods).

```
# Demonstrating an Update operation with SQLAlchemy
profile = User.query.filter_by(username='alice_doe').first()
profile.email = 'new.email@example.com'
db.session.commit()
```

Operation to Delete

Eliminating records from the database requires identifying the specific record(s) to be removed and executing a command (such as a DELETE statement or ORM method) to expunge the data from the table.

```
# Demonstrating a Delete operation with SQLAlchemy
profile = User.query.filter_by(username='alice_doe').first()
db.session.delete(profile)
db.session.commit()
```

Recommended Practices for CRUD Operations

To optimize the execution of CRUD operations and ensure robust data interactions, adhering to several best practices is recommended:

- Data Verification: Before creating or updating records, it's pivotal to verify the data to prevent the incorporation of invalid or malicious data into the database.

- Transaction Handling: Employing transactional mechanisms, particularly for intricate operations that involve multiple steps, ensures data consistency by allowing for rollbacks if errors occur.

- Security Measures: Enforcing security protocols such as sanitizing inputs and adhering to minimal privilege principles is essential for mitigating vulnerabilities like SQL injection.

- Optimizing Queries: Designing queries to be as streamlined as possible, such as by limiting the data fetched, aids in enhancing application performance and resource efficiency.

Conclusion

CRUD operations form the bedrock of database interaction within web applications, enabling seamless data creation, access, modification, and deletion. Proficiency in these operations equips developers to craft applications that adeptly manage data, maintaining the application's integrity and responsiveness. By following best practices in data handling, transaction oversight, security, and query efficiency, the efficacy of CRUD operations can be maximized. Through adept management of CRUD operations, developers ensure their applications are functional, secure, and user-friendly, capably managing the data lifecycle within the application.

Chapter Six

User Authentication

Implementing user registration and login

Establishing user registration and login features is a pivotal element in crafting secure and interactive web environments. These components not only enable a tailored user experience but also serve as the basis for access management and customization within applications. By facilitating user sign-up and authentication, web platforms can deliver personalized content, store user preferences, and safeguard confidential data. This narrative delves into the essential considerations, methodologies, and established practices for devising reliable user registration and authentication mechanisms.

User Sign-Up Process

The user sign-up procedure entails gathering crucial user details, such as usernames, email addresses, and passwords, and securely storing this data in the application's database. Key stages in this process include:

1. Displaying a Sign-Up Form: Showcasing a form that requests user information. This form should be intuitively designed, prioritizing ease of use and accessibility to ensure a smooth user journey.

2. Validating Input Data: Conducting both client-side and server-side checks to confirm that user-provided

information adheres to specific standards, such as password robustness and email format adherence. This validation is crucial for upholding data integrity and averting common security loopholes.

3. Secure Password Management: It is vital to handle passwords with utmost security. Storing passwords in plaintext is a significant vulnerability; instead, passwords should undergo cryptographic hashing, utilizing strong algorithms like bcrypt, before database storage. Enforcing password complexity rules can further bolster security.

4. User Account Verification: An advisable step is to authenticate the user's email or phone through a verification code or link. This measure validates the user's identity and aids in account recovery procedures.

5. Providing Feedback and Confirmation: Offering users clear guidance throughout the sign-up phase and acknowledging successful registration enhances the user experience, typically through a confirmation message or welcome email.

User Authentication

The authentication phase verifies user credentials against stored data, enabling user login. This phase typically involves:

1. Presenting a Login Form: Offering a login interface that solicits the user's username or email and password. The design of this form is critical to ensuring a positive user experience.

2. Credential Validation: After form submission, the application should compare the provided password against the stored hash in the database. Tools like Flask-Login simplify session management and common authentication tasks.

3. Session Creation: Successful authentication should lead to session initiation for the user. Sessions maintain the user's state across requests, preserving the logged-in status. Secure session handling is paramount to prevent vulnerabilities like session hijacking.

4. Managing Login Errors: Delivering secure and non-revealing error messages during login failures is essential. Messages should be generic to prevent information disclosure about username or password validity.

5. Enhancing Security Measures: Adding security layers, such as two-factor authentication (2FA) and locking accounts after several failed login attempts, significantly improves login security.

Best Practices

- HTTPS Enforcement: Ensure the encryption of data transmitted during registration and login by using HTTPS, safeguarding against interception and man-in-the-middle attacks.

- Implementing Rate Limiting: Applying rate limiting on sign-up and login routes helps mitigate brute force attacks.

- CSRF Defense: Incorporate anti-CSRF tokens in forms to counter Cross-Site Request Forgery attacks.

- Clear User Guidance: Provide explicit instructions and feedback during the registration and login phases, ensuring error messages do not expose sensitive details.

- Conducting Security Reviews: Periodically reassess and update the registration and authentication processes to tackle new vulnerabilities and adhere to evolving security standards.

Conclusion

Incorporating user registration and login capabilities is crucial for developing personalized and secure web applications. By following best practices in interface design, data validation, password security, and session management, developers can establish strong authentication systems that protect user data and enhance user interaction. Continuously revising these systems to address emerging security challenges is vital for maintaining the security and reliability of web applications. Through meticulous planning and implementation, user registration and login frameworks can lay a solid foundation for secure and user-focused web applications.

Managing user sessions

Administering user sessions is a pivotal component in the architecture of web applications, pivotal for ensuring a coherent and secure interaction for users. User sessions facilitate the persistence of state and user-specific information across numerous requests, enabling the application to render tailored content and interactions without necessitating continuous re-authentication by the user. Proficient session management is indispensable for upholding security standards, augmenting the user experience, and guaranteeing the application's scalability. This discourse aims to dissect the nuances of user session management, exploring its foundational principles, execution strategies, and the established norms for optimal management.

Fundamentals of User Sessions

A user session denotes a transient period of interaction between an individual and a web application, typically commencing with user login and concluding upon user logout or following a duration of inactivity. Sessions are employed to retain information such as user settings, authentication status, and contents of a shopping cart, thereby allowing the application to recall this data across various pages and requests.

Sessions are generally orchestrated through session identifiers (IDs) that are stored within cookies on the user's browser. Each time a request is made by the user, the session ID is transmitted to the server, enabling the application to access the corresponding session data and deliver a personalized response.

Establishing User Sessions

The establishment of user sessions encompasses several critical steps:

1. Initiation of Session: Following user authentication, a distinctive session ID is generated and retained on the server. This ID is also dispatched to the user's browser, typically in the form of a cookie, for inclusion in subsequent requests.

2. Storing Session Data: The data pertaining to a session can be housed in various locations, such as server memory, databases, or specialized session stores, with the selection influenced by scalability, performance, and security considerations.

3. Retrieving Session Data: For each user request, the application retrieves the session ID from the cookie and utilizes it to fetch the relevant session data stored on the server or within the session store.

4. Session Expiry: It is crucial to define an expiry for sessions to prevent the perpetuation of inactive sessions. This can be managed through session timeout settings and the periodic regeneration of session IDs.

5. Termination of Session: Sessions should be conclusively terminated upon user logout, entailing the removal of session data from the server or session store and the eradication of the session cookie from the user's browser.

Optimal Practices in Session Management

Effective session management necessitates adherence to a series of best practices:

- Securing Session IDs: Session IDs should be concocted using secure, random methodologies to thwart predictability and session hijacking. It's also pivotal to regenerate session IDs during significant events, like login, to counter fixation attacks.

- **Ensuring Cookie Security**: Session cookies ought to be flagged as `HttpOnly` and `Secure` to inhibit client-side script access and guarantee transmission exclusively over HTTPS, respectively. The `SameSite` attribute can also be set to mitigate CSRF attacks.

- Implementing Session Expiry and Timeouts: Establishing suitable session expiration and inactivity timeouts is essential for minimizing unauthorized access risks from dormant sessions.

- Safeguarding Session Data: Sensitive session data must be encrypted during transmission and storage to prevent disclosure in the event of interception or unauthorized access.

- Scalability Measures: For high-traffic applications or those deployed across distributed systems, utilizing a centralized session store like Redis or Memcached ensures the accessibility of session data across multiple application instances.

Contemporary Session Management Paradigms

With the shift towards stateless architectures and microservices, traditional session management practices are being complemented with token-based authentication methods, such as JSON Web Tokens (JWT), which encapsulate user identity and claims, facilitating stateless authentication and authorization across distributed components. Nonetheless, session-based authentication continues to be widely employed, especially in monolithic architectures or scenarios where session data is integral to application functionality.

Conclusion

The administration of user sessions is foundational to crafting web applications that are both interactive and secure, offering users a seamless experience while safeguarding against prevalent security threats. By proficiently managing session initiation, storage, retrieval, expiration, and termination, developers can enhance the user experience and maintain the application's security and scalability. Observing best practices in session management, including secure ID generation, cookie security, session expiration, and data protection, is paramount for preserving the integrity and efficiency of web applications. As the landscape of web development evolves, integrating conventional session management with contemporary authentication techniques offers a comprehensive approach to user session handling, meeting the diverse demands of modern web applications.

Password hashing and security best practices

Securing passwords through hashing and adhering to rigorous security protocols is essential in protecting user data and maintaining the integrity of online platforms. As the complexity of cyber threats escalates, implementing advanced password safeguarding measures is crucial to defend user accounts against unauthorized access and potential breaches. This treatise explores the principle of password hashing, investigates various hashing algorithms, and prescribes exemplary practices for ensuring password security in the context of web development.

The Principle of Password Hashing

Password hashing acts as a fundamental security measure, transforming plaintext passwords into a string of characters of a predetermined length, known as a "hash." This conversion process is irreversible, making it challenging to revert the hashed password back to its original plaintext form. Hashing ensures that, even in the event of a data breach, the compromised password data does not readily disclose the actual user passwords.

Algorithms for Password Hashing

There exists a range of algorithms employed for the purpose of password hashing, each characterized by its unique features and considerations:

- **BCrypt**: Renowned for its robustness in securing passwords, BCrypt inherently includes a salt (a random factor) to fend off rainbow table attacks and possesses a tunable "work factor," enabling the adjustment of the algorithm's computational intensity over time to offset advancements in processing power.

- **Argon2**: Celebrated as the champion of the Password Hashing Competition in 2015, Argon2 is offered in two forms, Argon2i and Argon2d, tailored to resist both side-channel attacks and attempts at GPU cracking. It integrates a salt and permits customization of iteration counts, memory footprint, and parallel processing capabilities.

- **PBKDF2** and **Scrypt**: These algorithms permit the customization of key lengths and iteration counts, allowing them to adapt to growing computational power. However, they are generally perceived to be less robust against GPU cracking efforts compared to Argon2.

Exemplary Practices for Password Security

Crafting a comprehensive approach to password security extends beyond selecting a potent hashing algorithm. The following practices are advocated:

1. Selection of Advanced Hashing Algorithms: Favor state-of-the-art, adaptable hashing algorithms like BCrypt, Argon2, PBKDF2, or Scrypt that incorporate a salt and are engineered to demand significant computational resources, thereby deterring brute-force attacks.

2. Utilization of Salts: Ensure each password hash is accompanied by a unique salt to protect against rainbow table attacks. Salts should be generated randomly and be of ample length to assure their distinctiveness.

3. Application of Key Stretching: Engage algorithms that facilitate key stretching, thereby intensifying the resource requirements for hash computation and enhancing resistance to brute-force attacks.

4. Implementation of Robust Password Policies: Enforce policies that promote the creation of strong, complex

passwords by stipulating minimum password lengths and the inclusion of diverse character types.

5. Assurance of Secure Password Transmission: Ensure the secure conveyance of passwords over networks by employing HTTPS, thwarting potential eavesdropping by malicious actors.

6. Rate Limiting and Account Lockout Measures: To counteract brute-force attacks, introduce rate limiting for login attempts and contemplate account lockouts or the necessity for additional verification after a series of unsuccessful login attempts.

7. Promotion of User Education: Provide users with guidance on formulating strong passwords and highlight the perils associated with reusing passwords across various sites and services.

8. Ongoing Revision of Security Protocols: Remain abreast of the latest developments in password security and hashing algorithms to ensure that your security measures are current and capable of countering contemporary threats.

9. Adoption of Multi-Factor Authentication (MFA): Where applicable, integrate MFA to introduce an additional layer of security beyond mere passwords, markedly elevating the level of account protection.

10. Routine Conduct of Security Audits: Systematically assess your password storage and authentication mechanisms to identify and rectify potential vulnerabilities.

Conclusion

The application of password hashing, combined with the observance of stringent password security measures, is indispensable for the preservation of user information and the sustenance of confidence in digital platforms. By leveraging sophisticated, flexible hashing algorithms, incorporating salts, mandating strict password standards, and staying informed of evolving security trends, developers can significantly diminish the likelihood of password-related security incidents. Further, enlightening users and embracing multi-factor authentication can substantially reinforce user account security. In the dynamically changing landscape of cyber threats, the persistent vigilance and adherence to best practices in password security are imperative for developers and organizations alike.

Chapter Seven

Flask Extensions

Introduction to popular Flask extensions

Flask stands out in the Python web framework landscape for its streamlined and adaptable nature, allowing for the seamless incorporation of a broad spectrum of functionalities through its rich ecosystem of extensions. These augmentations equip developers with an array of advanced features, from intricate database management and efficient form processing to sophisticated user authentication mechanisms, all while keeping Flask's core architecture uncluttered. This narrative introduces a selection of prominent Flask extensions, highlighting their functionalities and their role in enriching Flask-based applications.

Flask-SQLAlchemy

This extension bridges Flask with SQLAlchemy, a potent ORM framework for Python, streamlining database interactions within Flask projects. It enables the articulation of database models in Python, facilitating database transactions without necessitating direct SQL commands. Flask-SQLAlchemy's compatibility with various database systems such as SQLite, MySQL, and PostgreSQL renders it a flexible tool for database management in Flask environments.

Flask-Migrate

Flask-Migrate addresses database migration needs within Flask applications using SQLAlchemy, employing Alembic for this purpose. It introduces version control to database schemas, enabling the generation of migration scripts that are applicable across different database environments. This feature is especially valuable for applying schema updates in collaborative development settings and for seamless migrations in production environments.

Flask-WTF

Enhancing Flask with WTForms capabilities, Flask-WTF offers a robust solution for form creation, input validation, and rendering, complete with CSRF protection. This extension streamlines form handling in Flask applications, improving both security and user interaction.

Flask-Login

Focusing on user session management, Flask-Login simplifies the integration of authentication features in Flask applications. It automates various authentication tasks, including user login and session maintenance, providing a versatile solution that works with diverse user models.

Flask-RESTful

Flask-RESTful is tailored for developers crafting REST APIs within Flask, advocating for simplicity and adherence to best practices in developing resource-oriented views. This extension is ideal for creating scalable and maintainable RESTful services in Flask.

Flask-Mail

Facilitating email communication within Flask applications, Flask-Mail supports a range of functionalities from sending simple text and HTML emails to handling attachments. Its configurability through Flask's settings makes it an essential tool for applications requiring email functionalities.

Flask-Cache

Now operating under the name Flask-Caching, this extension introduces caching capabilities to Flask, significantly enhancing application performance by caching the output of computationally intensive operations. It supports various caching backends, including in-memory storage and distributed caching systems like Redis and Memcached.

Flask-Babel

Flask-Babel adds internationalization and localization features to Flask applications, enabling the adaptation of applications to multiple languages and regional formats for dates, numbers, and currencies. It is pivotal for developers targeting a worldwide audience.

Flask-Security

Integrating functionalities from Flask-Login, Flask-WTF, and Flask-Principal, Flask-Security offers a comprehensive security solution for Flask applications. It covers a range of security aspects, from user authentication and role-based authorization to password encryption and session management.

Conclusion

The extension ecosystem surrounding Flask substantially extends its utility, allowing developers to integrate a diverse set of features into their applications without compromising the simplicity and efficiency of Flask's core. Leveraging these key extensions, developers can elevate their Flask projects, incorporating sophisticated functionalities while maintaining the framework's inherent elegance and modularity. The ongoing expansion of Flask's extension ecosystem continues to solidify its status as a preferred choice among Python developers for building lightweight yet powerful web applications.

Integrating Flask extensions into your application

Incorporating Flask extensions into a web application is a strategic approach to enriching its features while maintaining the lightweight framework that Flask is known for. Flask's "micro" nature doesn't imply limitations but rather a streamlined core that's expandable with a variety of functionalities through extensions. This discussion aims to guide you through the seamless integration of Flask extensions into your application, emphasizing key practices and considerations to ensure effective augmentation.

Flask Extensions Overview

Flask extensions are essentially packages or modules designed to add specific capabilities to a Flask application, from ORM and database migrations to form handling and user authentication. These extensions are crafted to integrate smoothly with Flask's workflow, enriching your application without complicating its structure.

Preparing Your Flask Environment

The initial step involves setting up a conducive Flask environment, which includes creating a virtual environment, installing Flask, and organizing your project's structure thoughtfully. A well-structured project simplifies the integration process and management of extensions.

Selecting Suitable Extensions

The Flask ecosystem offers an array of extensions, making it crucial to choose those that align with your project's needs. Consider aspects like the extension's stability, community support, and compatibility with your Flask version to ensure you pick the most fitting options.

Integration Process

The process of integrating a Flask extension typically involves a few consistent steps, although specific actions might vary based on the extension's functionality:

1. Installation: Utilize a package manager like pip to install the chosen extension, and include it in your project's requirements.txt file for efficient dependency management.

2. Initialization: Import the extension into your Flask application and initialize it. This is often done using the factory pattern, where an extension instance is created

and then initialized with the Flask app object, either directly or within a factory function.

```python
from flask_sqlalchemy import SQLAlchemy

db = SQLAlchemy()

def create_app(config_filename):
    app = Flask(__name__)
    app.config.from_pyfile(config_filename)

    db.init_app(app)

    return app
```

3. Configuration: Set the required configuration variables specific to the extension in your Flask app's configuration section.

4. Utilization: Employ the extension's features in your application code, whether it's defining models with Flask-SQLAlchemy, creating forms with Flask-WTF, or managing user sessions with Flask-Login.

Integration Best Practices

- Comprehensive Documentation Review: Delve into the extension's documentation to grasp its setup, usage, and best practices fully. Well-documented extensions often provide adaptable examples.

- Extension Updates: Keep the extensions updated to leverage security enhancements, bug fixes, and new features, ensuring they remain compatible with your application.

- Code Isolation: Maintain a clean architecture by isolating extension-specific code, such as keeping database models in a dedicated module when using Flask-SQLAlchemy.

- Integration Testing: Conduct thorough testing post-integration to confirm the extension's functionality within your application, using automated tests for stability assurance.

- Performance Monitoring: Be mindful of the impact extensions might have on your application's performance, optimizing as necessary to maintain efficiency.

Troubleshooting Integration Challenges

Integration challenges can stem from version conflicts, configuration errors, or extension clashes. Addressing these issues typically involves:

- Consulting the extension's issue tracker for similar challenges faced by others.

- Ensuring compatibility with your Flask version.

- Double-checking configuration settings for accuracy.

- Engaging with the Flask community or extension maintainers for unresolved issues.

Conclusion

Enhancing your Flask application with extensions is a strategic way to introduce sophisticated functionalities while preserving Flask's streamlined essence. By judiciously selecting extensions, adhering to integration protocols, and following established best practices, you can effectively extend your application's capabilities. Regular updates, strategic code isolation, and rigorous testing are crucial for maintaining a functional, scalable, and efficient Flask application. Through thoughtful integration of Flask extensions, your application evolves into a more comprehensive and dynamic web platform, adept at catering to a broad spectrum of user needs.

Customizing extensions to fit your needs

Tailoring Flask extensions to align with the unique demands of a project is a nuanced aspect of web development, especially within the versatile Flask framework known for its expansive ecosystem of plug-ins. These extensions inherently provide broad functionalities that accelerate the development workflow. Nonetheless, the intricacies of certain projects necessitate refining these extensions to ensure they dovetail with the project's specific requirements or mesh seamlessly with the application's existing architecture. This exposition focuses on methodologies for adeptly adapting Flask extensions, ensuring they not only contribute enhanced capabilities but also resonate with the particular needs of your application.

The Essence of Extension Adaptation

Adapting an extension involves modifying its default operation, configurations, or integration approach to cater to specific application requirements. This can range from straightforward configuration adjustments to more intricate changes that involve augmenting or supplanting the extension's core components.

Evaluating Adaptation Requirements

Prior to embarking on adaptation, it's imperative to scrutinize the necessity and extent of the modifications needed. Determine whether simple configuration alterations suffice or if deeper modifications are warranted. Assess the implications of these changes on maintenance, subsequent updates, and their interplay with other application components.

Adaptation Techniques

Configurational Adjustments

A multitude of Flask extensions come equipped with an array of configurable parameters that permit significant adaptation without necessitating alterations to the extension's codebase. Delve into the extension's documentation to uncover configurable options and utilize them to mold the extension's functionality to your preferences.

Class Subclassing

For nuanced adaptation, consider subclassing the extension's classes. This technique allows for the inheritance of functionality from the original extension while introducing bespoke modifications or enhancements. Subclassing proves particularly beneficial when you aim to tweak specific methods or append new methods to an extension's classes.

```python
from flask_login import LoginManager

class EnhancedLoginManager(LoginManager):
    def __init__(self, *args, **kwargs):
        super(EnhancedLoginManager, self).__init__(*args, **kwargs)
        # Custom initialization or method overrides

    def augment_login_view(self):
        # Customized method to refine login view behavior
```

Extension Wrapping

Constructing a wrapper around an extension serves as an alternative adaptation strategy. This entails crafting a new class or function that internally utilizes the extension while offering a customized interface or additional features. Wrapping is advantageous for amalgamating multiple extensions or reshaping their interfaces for more organic integration into your application.

Direct Extension Modification (Forking)

When extensive adaptations are necessitated, directly modifying the extension's code by forking its repository might be the most viable option. While this approach grants the utmost flexibility, it also escalates the maintenance burden, necessitating manual integration of updates from the original extension and ensuring ongoing compatibility.

Optimal Practices for Extension Adaptation

- Limit Modifications: Aim for minimalistic changes to ease the upkeep and minimize the efforts required for future extension updates.

- Comprehensive Documentation: Meticulously document all adaptations, elucidating the rationale behind the changes and any potential repercussions on the application's functionality.

- Segregation: Segregate adapted extensions or components within a distinct module in your project to clearly demarcate them from the standard application code.

- Rigorous Testing: Implement exhaustive tests for adapted components to ascertain that modifications do not introduce defects or regressions.

- Community Contributions: If your adaptations address widespread use cases, contemplate contributing them to the extension's community. This could lead to the integration of your adaptations in subsequent releases, diminishing the necessity for local modifications.

Navigating Updates and Compatibility

Adapting extensions introduces challenges in maintaining congruence with future updates of the extension. To navigate these challenges:

- Stay Informed on Updates: Regularly monitor for new releases of the original extension and peruse release notes to discern changes that might impact your adaptations.

- Compatibility Assessments: Prior to updating an adapted extension, thoroughly evaluate the new version in a testing environment to pinpoint and rectify any compatibility issues.

- Extension Contributions: Should your adaptations fulfill common requirements, consider contributing them to the extension's repository. This could lead to their inclusion in future versions, reducing the necessity for bespoke modifications.

Conclusion

Refining Flask extensions to meet specific project imperatives is a valuable practice in web development, enabling the precise customization of functionalities to resonate with application requirements. By employing strategies such as configurational adjustments, subclassing, wrapping, or direct code modification, developers can ensure extensions serve their intended purposes effectively. Adhering to best practices in adaptation, like minimal changes, detailed documentation, and isolated testing, is essential for upholding a maintainable and update-friendly codebase. Engaging with the extension's community and contributing back can also enrich the ecosystem, potentially diminishing the need for future customizations.

Chapter Eight

Building RESTful APIs

Understanding RESTful principles

Grasping the fundamentals of RESTful principles is essential for the contemporary development of web services and applications. Originating from the architectural style termed Representational State Transfer, coined by Roy Fielding in his 2000 doctoral dissertation, REST has emerged as the predominant framework for crafting networked applications, attributed to its straightforwardness, scalability, and efficient performance. This exposition ventures into the foundational principles of REST, elucidates its defining constraints, and examines how these tenets contribute to the creation of effective, reliable, and scalable web services.

Foundational Concepts of REST

At the heart of REST lies the concept of resources, which are entities that can be identified and expressed in data form. In RESTful systems, resources are manipulated via a consistent set of stateless operations, with a clear distinction made between the resources and the representations sent back to the client. This methodology offers several advantages, including modular architecture, enhanced scalability, and a distinct separation of concerns.

Principal Constraints of REST

REST's architectural style is characterized by six principal constraints that dictate the design and interaction of components within a RESTful ecosystem. These constraints encompass:

1. Client-Server Structure: RESTful applications adhere to a client-server framework that delineates concerns, facilitating the independent evolution of client and server components. The client is responsible for the user interface and state, whereas the server manages data storage and stateless operations.

2. Stateless Communication: Every client request to a server is self-contained, carrying all necessary information for the server to process and respond to the request. This absence of client session state on the server side promotes scalability and reliability.

3. Cachability: REST enables responses to be explicitly marked as either cacheable or non-cacheable, enhancing network efficiency. Cacheable responses allow client-side caches to reuse response data for equivalent future responses, diminishing the frequency of server requests.

4. Uniform Interface: A fundamental tenet of REST is the uniform interface between components, which simplifies the architecture and improves interaction visibility. This includes guidelines for resource identification, representation-based manipulation, self-descriptive messages, and the utilization of hypermedia as the engine of application state (HATEOAS).

5. Layered System Architecture: REST supports a layered system design where components interact with only their immediate layer, obscuring the larger system architecture. This enhances scalability through mechanisms like load balancing and caching and bolsters security by constraining component behavior.

6. Code on Demand (Optional): This optional constraint permits servers to augment client functionality by transmitting executable code, offering flexibility in reducing initial client-side feature requirements.

Crafting RESTful Services

The implementation of RESTful services centers on defining resources, their URIs (Uniform Resource Identifiers), and employing standard HTTP methods for resource interaction: GET, POST, PUT, DELETE, and PATCH. These methods correspond with CRUD (Create, Read, Update, Delete) operations commonly found in persistent storage systems, ensuring a consistent and intuitive approach to API development.

Advantages of a RESTful Approach

Adopting a RESTful design yields numerous benefits for web services, including:

- Scalability: The separation of client and server responsibilities, coupled with stateless communication, allows RESTful services to scale more efficiently.

- Simplicity: Utilizing standard HTTP methods for resource interactions simplifies API design, making services more intuitive and predictable.

- Adaptability: RESTful services can provide resource representations in various formats, such as JSON, XML, or HTML, catering to diverse client needs.

- Performance Enhancements: Caching capabilities reduce redundant data transmissions, optimizing network communication efficiency.

- Client Application Portability: The decoupling of the user interface from the data layer enables client applications to be portable across different platforms.

Conclusion

A thorough understanding and application of RESTful principles are pivotal in the creation of web services that are not only scalable and efficient but also maintainable. By adhering to REST's defined constraints and leveraging standard HTTP protocols, developers can forge web services that offer robust performance, scalability, and adaptability. As the digital landscape continues to evolve, the principles underpinning REST retain their relevance, guiding the architecture of web services adept at navigating the complexities of the networked world.

Creating API endpoints with Flask

Crafting API endpoints using Flask entails the development and configuration of routes that manage HTTP requests and deliver responses in formats like JSON, which are readily utilized by client applications. Flask, recognized for its minimalistic yet extensible architecture, is particularly adept for constructing RESTful APIs, thanks to its straightforward syntax, adaptability, and a rich selection of supplementary extensions. This discourse aims to navigate through the intricacies of establishing API endpoints within Flask, offering insights into fundamental concepts, established practices, and illustrative examples to aid developers in forging effective, scalable, and well-maintained APIs.

Core Concepts of API Endpoints in Flask

API endpoints serve as designated URIs within a web application, functioning as gateways to access various resources or services. Flask facilitates the definition of these endpoints through the `@app.route` decorator, associating URIs with Python functions known as view functions. These functions are tasked with processing incoming requests and crafting corresponding responses.

Initiating a Flask Application

The initial step in endpoint creation involves setting up a foundational Flask application. This setup includes Flask installation, initializing an application instance, and structuring the project to segregate configurations, routes, and business logic, thereby enhancing the application's manageability.

```
from flask import Flask

app = Flask(__name__)

@app.route('/')
def welcome():
    return 'Welcome to the API!'
```

Crafting RESTful API Endpoints

Designing API endpoints demands adherence to RESTful conventions, ensuring that URIs represent specific resources and that HTTP methods (GET, POST, PUT, DELETE) directly map to operations (read, create, update, delete) on those resources.

Formulating API Endpoints in Flask

Managing HTTP Methods

Flask enables the handling of diverse HTTP methods within routes by specifying the `methods` parameter in the `@app.route` decorator. Utilize Flask's `request` object to access incoming data and the `jsonify` function for generating JSON-formatted responses.

```python
from flask import Flask, request, jsonify

app = Flask(__name__)

@app.route('/api/resources', methods=['GET', 'POST'])
def resources():
    if request.method == 'GET':
        # Fetch and return resources
        pass
    elif request.method == 'POST':
        # Instantiate a new resource
        data = request.json
        # Process and store the new resource
        return jsonify(data), 201
```

Dynamic Routes

Flask supports the creation of dynamic routes with variable segments, enhancing endpoint versatility and descriptiveness. Employ angle brackets **<variable>** to denote variable segments within the URI, which are then accessible as parameters in the associated view function.

```python
@app.route('/api/resources/<int:resource_id>', methods=['GET', 'PUT', 'DELETE'])
def single_resource(resource_id):
    if request.method == 'GET':
        # Retrieve and return the specified resource
        pass
    elif request.method == 'PUT':
        # Update the specified resource
        pass
    elif request.method == 'DELETE':
        # Remove the specified resource
        pass
```

Established Practices for API Development in Flask

- Utilization of HTTP Status Codes: Employ precise HTTP status codes to clearly communicate the results of requests, enhancing the API's intelligibility and user-friendliness.

- Error Management: Implement comprehensive error handling to gracefully address and respond to exceptions, providing informative error messages and appropriate status codes.

- Data Validation: Ensure the validation of incoming data to confirm its adherence to expected formats and constraints, bolstering the API's dependability and security.

- Securing Endpoints: Safeguard your API through authentication and authorization measures, such as token-based access control, to regulate resource access.

- API Documentation: Thoroughly document your API endpoints, elucidating the available methods, request parameters, response structures, and status codes to aid both client integration and developer understanding.

Conclusion

Developing API endpoints with Flask presents a streamlined and potent method for constructing web APIs. By embracing RESTful design principles, accommodating various HTTP methods, and enabling dynamic routes, developers can create versatile and efficient APIs. Observing best practices, including the judicious use of HTTP status codes, meticulous error handling, input validation, and endpoint security, further elevates the caliber and safeguarding of Flask APIs. Flask's simplicity and extensibility equip developers to produce APIs that are not only operational but also scalable and maintainable, meeting a broad spectrum of application needs.

Handling request and response data

Mastering the management of request and response data stands as a fundamental aspect of crafting dynamic web applications. This entails adeptly receiving client-sent data, processing it in line with the application's logic, and dispatching suitable responses back to the client. The seamless orchestration of this data interchange is essential for the operational integrity, performance, and user engagement of web platforms. This discourse examines strategies and established practices for the efficient management of request and response data, emphasizing the server-side handling.

Deciphering Request Data

Data from client requests manifests in several formats, including URL parameters, query strings, request bodies, and headers, each serving distinct purposes:

- URL Parameters: Employed to pinpoint specific resources or transmit minimal data within the URL itself.

- Query Strings: Attached to the URL's end, facilitating the conveyance of supplementary data for processing.

- Request Bodies: Host more substantial data within POST or PUT requests, commonly in JSON, XML, or form-encoded formats.

- Headers: Convey request metadata, such as content type, authentication credentials, and client specifics.

Managing Request Data

The server's role in managing request data involves extracting and validating the incoming data prior to any processing actions or database interactions. Web frameworks like Flask and Express provide inherent functionalities to access and parse request data components:

- Data Extraction: Harness framework-specific functionalities or middleware to parse query strings,

URL parameters, and request bodies. For instance, Flask's request object and Express's `req` object offer straightforward access to these data elements.

- Data Validation: Critical to ensure incoming data adheres to expected formats and standards, safeguarding the application from erroneous or harmful data inputs. Tools such as Joi (JavaScript) or Marshmallow (Python) aid in implementing comprehensive data validation protocols.

Constructing Responses

Subsequent to processing the request data, the server is tasked with formulating a response to relay back to the client. Responses generally comprise a status code, headers, and a response body:

- Status Codes: Reflect the request's outcome, with typical codes like 200 (OK), 404 (Not Found), and 500 (Internal Server Error).

- Response Headers: Offer metadata about the response, detailing aspects like content type and caching directives.

- Response Body: Delivers the actual response content, often in JSON format for API endpoints, or HTML for standard web pages.

Data Handling Best Practices

- Framework Utilization: Capitalize on the web framework's built-in tools and utilities for request data parsing and response generation, ensuring code simplicity and adherence to best practices.

- Content Adaptation: Implement content adaptation to dynamically provide varied response formats (JSON, XML, HTML) based on the request's Accept header, augmenting API versatility.

- Robust Error Management: Establish a comprehensive error management framework to capture and handle exceptions, log errors, and return descriptive error messages with relevant HTTP status codes.

- Security Protocols: Enforce security best practices like input sanitization to defend against injection threats and guarantee the proper encryption or anonymization of sensitive response data.

- Optimizing Performance: Enhance response data efficiency by reducing payload sizes and optimizing loading times, employing strategies like data compression and pagination for extensive data sets.

Conclusion

Efficiently managing request and response data is a keystone in the development of web applications, shaping the client-server interaction. Through insightful management of incoming request data and leveraging framework capabilities for data parsing and validation, developers can ensure secure and effective data processing. Crafting well-defined responses, marked by precise status codes and informative content, completes the communication loop, furnishing clients with necessary feedback or data. Adhering to best practices in data management, security, and performance fine-tuning further enhances the process, resulting in robust, engaging, and secure web applications. As web technology continues to advance, maintaining abreast of the latest methodologies and tools for request and response management remains imperative for developers aiming to deliver superior web solutions.

Chapter Nine

Error Handling and Debugging

Configuring custom error pages

Setting up tailored error pages is a vital component of web development, playing a key role in enhancing user interaction by providing clear, user-centric feedback during error occurrences. Custom error pages replace generic or obscure error messages with content that is informative and aligned with the website's aesthetic, offering navigational cues or even light-hearted content to mitigate user frustration. This discourse delves into the significance of tailored error pages, outlines methodologies for their configuration, and highlights practices for optimal utility.

The Significance of Tailored Error Pages

Tailored error pages fulfill several critical roles within a web application:

- Elevating User Interaction: By maintaining the website's design consistency, custom error pages ensure a seamless user experience, even in error scenarios.

- Providing Constructive Guidance: These pages can clarify the nature of the error and suggest subsequent actions, such as navigating back to the main site or reaching out to support.

- Opportunities for Branding: Error pages present a unique opportunity to reinforce brand identity, transforming potential negative encounters into positive brand interactions.

- SEO Benefits: Properly configured custom error pages, particularly 404 pages, can aid in preserving the website's SEO integrity by preventing search engines from indexing invalid links.

Configuration of Tailored Error Pages

The approach to setting up custom error pages varies with the web server or development framework in use. Below are configurations for common environments:

For Apache Web Servers

With Apache, custom error pages are set via the `.htaccess` file, using the `ErrorDocument` directive to define specific pages for different HTTP status codes:

```
ErrorDocument 404 /404.html
ErrorDocument 500 /500.html
```

This setup instructs Apache to serve `/404.html` for 404 Not Found errors and `/500.html` for 500 Internal Server Error occurrences.

For Nginx Web Servers

In Nginx, custom error pages are specified within the server block in the `nginx.conf` file, assigning specific error pages to certain status codes:

```
error_page 404 /404.html;
error_page 500 502 503 504 /50x.html;
```

This configuration directs Nginx to use `/404.html` for 404 errors and `/50x.html` for errors in the 500 range.

For Flask Framework

Flask facilitates custom error page setup through the `errorhandler` decorator, allowing the creation of view functions that render specific templates for various error codes:

```
from flask import Flask, render_template

app = Flask(__name__)

@app.errorhandler(404)
def not_found_error(e):
    return render_template('404.html'), 404

@app.errorhandler(500)
def server_error(e):
    return render_template('500.html'), 500
```

Practices for Optimal Custom Error Pages

- Prioritize User-Friendliness: Design error pages that are straightforward and empathetic, steering clear of technical jargon.

- Incorporate Navigation Aids: Embed links to important pages like the homepage or support contacts to assist users in finding their way.

- Monitor Error Page Hits: Use tracking on error pages to identify and address recurring issues.

- Maintain Lightweight Error Pages: Ensure error pages are independent of potentially problematic resources such as external scripts or styles.

- Conduct Thorough Testing: Regularly test error pages to confirm their proper display under various conditions and on multiple devices.

Conclusion

Custom error pages are indispensable in web development, significantly improving user experiences during error events. By configuring custom error pages on your web server or within your development framework, you can offer users helpful guidance, reinforce your branding, and even convert a negative user experience into a positive one. Adhering to best practices in error page design and configuration ensures they are effective, user-friendly, and supportive of your site's overall usability and search engine optimization efforts. As web technologies advance, strategies for custom error pages may evolve, yet their role in elevating the user experience will remain crucial.

Debugging Flask applications

Troubleshooting Flask applications is an essential phase in the development lifecycle, aimed at detecting and rectifying problems that hinder the app's functionality or efficiency. Given Flask's stature as a minimalist yet adaptable Python web framework, it offers a suite of tools and methodologies conducive to effective troubleshooting, enabling developers to swiftly isolate and amend errors, thereby refining their code. This narrative delves into the methodologies for efficient troubleshooting within Flask applications, encompassing Flask's inherent debugging capabilities, auxiliary tools, and established practices to streamline the troubleshooting process.

Inherent Debugger in Flask

Flask is equipped with a robust internal debugger that becomes operational when the application operates in a development setting. This debugger renders detailed error pages upon encountering exceptions, showcasing stack traces, request details, and interactive Python consoles for each stack frame, thereby facilitating error analysis. To activate the Flask debugger, ensure the application is executed with `debug` set to `**True**`:

```
app.run(debug=True)
```

It's imperative to deactivate debug mode in production environments to safeguard sensitive data.

Implementing Logging

Logging plays a pivotal role in troubleshooting Flask applications. Leveraging Python's native `**logging**` module, Flask can log messages, configurable to capture a wide spectrum of data from critical errors and exceptions to verbose debugging information. Establishing structured logging aids in mapping the application's operational flow and pinpointing areas of concern:

```
import logging

logging.basicConfig(level=logging.DEBUG)
app.logger.info('Application initiated')
```

Logs can be directed towards various outputs such as console, files, or dedicated logging services for in-depth monitoring and diagnostics.

Flask Extensions for Enhanced Troubleshooting

A plethora of Flask extensions are available that augment the troubleshooting experience by introducing additional tools and functionalities:

- Flask-DebugToolbar: This extension introduces a dynamic debug toolbar to the Flask app, offering insights into aspects like request parameters, headers, cookies, SQL queries, etc. It proves invaluable in decoding the application's workings and identifying performance bottlenecks.

- Flask-Profiler: Flask-Profiler delivers performance profiling based on endpoints, enabling the identification of sluggish endpoints and the analysis of their execution times.

Incorporating these extensions can significantly facilitate the diagnosis of issues and the enhancement of application performance.

Troubleshooting with IDEs

Integrated Development Environments (IDEs) such as PyCharm, Visual Studio Code, or Eclipse with PyDev, present sophisticated troubleshooting capabilities, including breakpoints, stepwise execution, variable inspection, and more. Configuring your Flask app within an IDE offers a more interactive and granular troubleshooting experience, aiding in the resolution of intricate issues.

Established Practices for Flask Application Troubleshooting

- Gradual Development and Testing: Embrace a phased approach to development and testing, validating new code in small segments. This strategy aids in isolating errors and simplifies the troubleshooting process.

- Comprehensive Testing: Employ thorough unit and integration tests using frameworks like pytest or unittest. Early testing can identify errors and confirm the functionality of individual components and their integration.

- Custom Error Handling: Craft custom error handling within Flask to gracefully log and manage exceptions. Bespoke error pages can not only enhance the user experience in error scenarios but also furnish developers with critical error insights.

- Error Replication in a Safe Environment: Strive to replicate errors within a safe development or staging environment. This allows for risk-free experimentation and troubleshooting without impacting live systems.

- Reference Flask and Extension Documentation: Flask's official documentation, along with that of any employed extensions, serves as a rich resource for grasping common troubleshooting tactics and issues. Online communities and platforms like Stack Overflow can also offer solutions to prevalent challenges.

Conclusion

Troubleshooting Flask applications effectively encompasses leveraging Flask's built-in debugging tools, structured logging, third-party extensions, and the functionalities of IDEs. By following these tools and practices such as phased development, exhaustive testing, and custom error management, developers can adeptly identify and rectify issues within their Flask apps. Furthermore, engaging with the Flask community and consulting documentation can offer supplementary support and insights throughout the troubleshooting journey. Keeping abreast of emerging troubleshooting tools and methodologies remains critical for sustaining robust, high-performing Flask applications in the evolving landscape of web development.

Logging and monitoring

In the domain of software engineering and systems management, the practices of logging and monitoring are paramount, providing vital visibility into the inner workings, performance, and overall health of applications and infrastructures. Logging encompasses the orderly recording of activities, events, and anomalies within systems, serving a multitude of purposes from debugging to compliance auditing.

Monitoring, on the other hand, entails the vigilant observation of these logs alongside crucial system metrics, facilitating the early detection and resolution of potential issues. This exploration delves into the nuances of logging and monitoring, underscoring their significance, methodologies for implementation, and optimal practices for leveraging these processes effectively.

The Essence of Logging

Logging constitutes the structured documentation of occurrences within a system, capturing key details such as the timing of events, their nature, severity, and associated context. This documentation aids in unraveling the sequence of actions leading to particular states or errors, thereby streamlining the diagnostic process.

Logging Varieties

- System Logs: Document the operational events within an application, detailing user interactions and the flow of business processes.

- Diagnostic Logs: Focus on capturing detailed error and exception information, crucial for the debugging process.

- Traffic Logs: Record all incoming server requests, noting essential details like requester information, requested resources, and the responses served.

- Compliance Logs: Keep track of events with security implications, aiding in security reviews and regulatory compliance.

The Imperatives of Monitoring

Beyond the analysis of log data, monitoring encompasses the continuous scrutiny of performance metrics and system states to ascertain the smooth functioning of services. It covers a gamut of metrics from basic resource utilization to advanced performance indicators, employing tools that provide real-time insights, alerts, and comprehensive data analysis to preempt and address service disruptions or degradations.

Monitoring Approaches

- Infrastructure Surveillance: Concentrates on the health and efficiency of hardware and network components.
- Performance Monitoring: Assesses the responsiveness and user experience of applications, focusing on metrics like load times and transaction success rates.
- Analytical Log Monitoring: Involves the real-time scrutiny of log entries to detect patterns, anomalies, and potential points of failure.

Instituting Logging and Monitoring

The establishment of robust logging and monitoring frameworks necessitates the selection of appropriate technologies, the delineation of key metrics and loggable events, and the seamless integration of these practices into the development and deployment lifecycles.

Logging Mechanisms

A plethora of tools and libraries exists to facilitate sophisticated logging practices, including:

- Dedicated Logging Libraries: Such as Log4j for Java and Python's native logging module, offering comprehensive facilities for log generation and management.

- Consolidated Logging Platforms: Solutions like the ELK Stack and Splunk provide centralized logging capabilities, enabling the aggregation, analysis, and visualization of logs from multiple sources.

Monitoring Technologies

The landscape of monitoring solutions spans from versatile open-source tools to all-encompassing commercial platforms, offering a range of functionalities from basic monitoring to advanced analytical insights:

- Community-Driven Tools: Prometheus, Grafana, and Nagios offer customizable and extensible monitoring solutions, backed by vibrant user communities.

- Integrated Monitoring Services: Platforms such as New Relic and Datadog deliver holistic monitoring suites, encompassing application performance insights, infrastructure health checks, and log analytics.

Optimal Practices in Logging and Monitoring

- Comprehensive Logging Strategies: Formulate and adhere to precise logging standards, specifying what events to log, preferred log formats, and data retention policies.

- Structured Log Formats: Employ structured log formats like JSON to ease the parsing and analysis of log data.

- Meaningful Alert Configurations: Design alerting mechanisms around critical metrics and thresholds to ensure that alerts remain relevant and actionable.

- Early Integration of Monitoring: Embed monitoring practices at the outset of development projects to facilitate early issue detection and baseline performance characterization.

- Routine Evaluation of Logs and Metrics: Periodically review logged data and monitoring outputs to refine alert configurations, enhance system performance, and bolster error handling protocols.

- Log Data Protection: Safeguard log information, especially logs containing sensitive data, ensuring alignment with applicable data protection standards.

Conclusion

The disciplines of logging and monitoring are foundational to the effective management, optimization, and safeguarding of software systems and infrastructures. Through meticulous logging and comprehensive monitoring, organizations can illuminate the operational dynamics of their systems, proactively mitigate risks, and optimize performance. Embracing best practices and deploying suitable technological solutions are crucial for establishing logging and monitoring systems that support continuous refinement and operational excellence. Remaining conversant with evolving trends and technologies in logging and monitoring is essential for professionals in software development and IT operations, ensuring the sustained reliability and performance of their digital ecosystems.

Chapter Ten

Testing Your Flask Application

Writing unit tests with Flask-Testing

Unit testing stands as a cornerstone of software development, enabling the validation of individual components within an application in isolation. For developers utilizing Flask, a renowned lightweight Python framework, the Flask-Testing extension enhances the framework's native testing capabilities, providing specialized tools for more effective and streamlined unit tests. This discussion delves into the nuances of crafting unit tests with Flask-Testing, detailing essential concepts, initialization steps, and recommended practices for achieving thorough testing coverage.

Overview of Flask-Testing

Flask-Testing augments the inherent testing features of Flask, introducing advanced functionalities tailored for Flask applications. It simplifies tasks such as configuring test environments, dispatching requests to Flask routes, and evaluating responses, thereby optimizing the unit testing process.

Initializing Flask-Testing

Embarking on unit testing with Flask-Testing involves installing the extension, establishing a test structure within your Flask project, and configuring a test environment. The initial steps include:

1. Installation: Flask-Testing is easily installable via pip:

```
pip install Flask-Testing
```

2. Configuring Test Settings: Within your Flask application, define a test-specific configuration that outlines parameters suitable for a testing scenario, like disabling certain protections or employing an in-memory database.

3. Creating a Test Case Class: Develop a class for your test cases by extending `TestCase` from Flask-Testing. This class will house methods for initializing and tearing down the test environment for each test function.

```python
from flask_testing import TestCase
from myapp import create_app, db

class MyAppTest(TestCase):

    def create_app(self):
        # Instantiate your Flask app with test configurations
        return create_app('test')

    def setUp(self):
        # Prepare the test environment prior to each test
        db.create_all()

    def tearDown(self):
        # Clean up the test environment post-test
        db.session.remove()
        db.drop_all()
```

Crafting Unit Tests

With the foundational test environment in place, you can proceed to compose unit tests for various functionalities within your Flask application. Adhering to the Arrange-Act-Assert pattern is advisable:

1. Arrange: Establish the prerequisites for your test, such as populating test data or adjusting the test setting.

2. Act: Invoke the functionality under test, often by issuing a request to a Flask endpoint.

3. Assert: Confirm the outcome aligns with expectations, utilizing Flask-Testing's assertion methods to validate response content, status codes, and more.

```python
def test_sample_endpoint(self):
    response = self.client.get('/sample')
    self.assertEqual(response.status_code, 200)
    self.assertIn('Sample Content', response.data)
```

Recommended Unit Testing Practices with Flask-Testing

- Test Isolation: Guarantee the independence of each test by utilizing `setUp` and `tearDown` for environment preparation and cleanup, ensuring tests do not influence each other.

- Comprehensive Coverage: Strive for extensive coverage by testing all crucial pathways and scenarios within your application. Coverage measurement tools can assist in identifying untested areas.

- Utilization of Mocks: Employ mocks to replicate the behavior of external dependencies, focusing tests on the component under scrutiny. Python's `unittest.mock` offers comprehensive mocking capabilities.

- Clarity and Descriptiveness: Craft tests with clear, descriptive names and include comments where necessary to elucidate test intentions and expected behaviors for other developers.

- Integration with Continuous Integration (CI): Embed unit testing within a CI pipeline to automate test execution upon code modifications, aiding in early problem detection.

Conclusion

Employing Flask-Testing for unit tests significantly bolsters the robustness and dependability of Flask-based applications. Through meticulous test setup, focused and isolated testing, and adherence to established best practices, developers can construct a solid suite of unit tests that not only facilitate early issue identification but also contribute to improved code design and application stability. Integrating unit testing into the development lifecycle not only aids in preempting potential problems but also fosters better architectural decisions, culminating in more resilient Flask applications. Keeping abreast of evolving testing techniques and tools remains essential for developers committed to crafting high-caliber Flask applications.

Testing views, forms, and models

Evaluating the functionality of views, forms, and models is a cornerstone practice in the realm of web application development, ensuring each segment operates seamlessly and interacts appropriately within the system's ecosystem. This examination focuses on the approach to rigorously test these critical components within frameworks like Flask and Django, emphasizing the importance of meticulous evaluation and shedding light on effective testing strategies.

Evaluating View Functions

View functions, orchestrating request handling and response delivery, are central to web applications' operational flow. To test views effectively:

1. Emulating Requests: Employ testing utilities or the framework's testing client to emulate various HTTP request types to the view endpoints, mimicking user or client interactions.

2. Validating Responses: Assess the response for the correct status code, headers, and content. Tools like BeautifulSoup can be instrumental for analyzing HTML responses from dynamic views.

3. Verifying Contextual Data: For views passing data to templates, it's crucial to ensure the accuracy and completeness of this contextual information, guaranteeing templates render as intended.

Assessing Forms

Forms play a pivotal role in user data input and validation. Thorough testing of forms is vital for:

1. Validation Accuracy: Conduct tests with a spectrum of input scenarios to confirm the form's validation logic robustly identifies valid and invalid submissions, providing clear feedback.

2. Submission Handling: Simulate form submissions to validate correct processing of valid entries, which might include database updates, redirections, or specific acknowledgments.

3. Edge Case Consideration: Incorporate tests for atypical input cases to ensure the application handles such data gracefully, safeguarding against unexpected or malicious submissions.

Inspecting Models

Models, delineating the data structure and encapsulating business logic, require thorough testing to ensure data integrity and logic accuracy.

1. Field Constraints: Examine model fields to validate enforcement of data types, constraints, and defaults by attempting to save invalid data and expecting appropriate exceptions.

2. Business Logic Verification: For models with embedded business logic in methods, devise unit tests that scrutinize these methods under diverse scenarios to affirm their reliability.

3. Inter-Model Relationships: In models with linkages to other models, such as foreign key relationships, test these connections for correctness and ensure related object queries yield the anticipated outcomes.

Effective Testing Practices for Views, Forms, and Models

- Automated Test Execution: Utilize frameworks like pytest for Python to script and automate tests, ensuring repeatability and ease of integration into continuous integration workflows.

- Independent Test Design: Structure tests to be self-contained, preventing the outcome of one test from influencing another, with proper setup and cleanup routines for each test case.

- Mocking for Isolation: Implement mocking to decouple the component under test from external systems or services, focusing the test on the component's intrinsic functionality.

- Aiming for Extensive Coverage: Strive for broad test coverage that spans typical use cases, boundary conditions, and error scenarios, prioritizing the depth and relevance of tests over mere coverage metrics.

- Maintainable Test Suites: Craft tests with descriptive naming and documentation, organizing them for clarity and ease of maintenance, enhancing the codebase's longevity and adaptability.

- Iterative Testing Integration: Embed testing within the development lifecycle, conducting tests regularly to identify and rectify issues promptly, with continuous integration tools facilitating automated testing upon each code revision.

Conclusion

The rigorous evaluation of views, forms, and models is paramount in crafting web applications that are both robust and dependable. Through strategic testing of these integral components, developers can assure the system's expected behavior under various scenarios, laying a solid foundation for user interaction and system stability. Adhering to best practices in testing automation, case isolation, and thorough coverage not only bolsters the testing regimen but also enhances the application's overall quality and maintainability. As the landscape of web development tools and methodologies evolves, remaining attuned to emerging testing practices is essential for developers dedicated to delivering superior web applications.

Introduction to integration testing

Integration testing stands as a crucial phase within the software testing lifecycle, aimed at evaluating the interactions and cohesiveness among various modules or components of an application. This testing phase transcends unit testing's scope by examining the interplay between different parts of the software, ensuring they function harmoniously. This exposition delves into the essence of integration testing, highlighting its significance, various approaches, and recommended practices for conducting these tests effectively.

Significance of Integration Testing

The primary goal of integration testing is to uncover any discrepancies or issues that may arise when different software modules interact, such as data inconsistency, communication errors, and workflow disruptions. Through this testing, developers can ensure that the assembled modules work together seamlessly, fulfilling the software's intended functionality and performance criteria.

Core Objectives

- Interface Defect Detection: Pinpointing problems that occur during the interaction between integrated components, including incorrect data handling or workflow interruptions.

- Functional Integrity Verification: Confirming that the integrated modules collectively deliver the expected functionality as a cohesive unit.

- Assessment of Performance and Stability: Evaluating how the system performs and remains stable under various conditions when multiple components interact.

Approaches to Integration Testing

Integration testing can be conducted using different strategies, each suited to specific project requirements and system structures:

1. Big Bang Approach: This method entails integrating and testing all components in one go, providing a straightforward but challenging scenario for isolating issues due to the simultaneous testing of all interfaces.

2. Incremental Testing: A more systematic approach, incremental testing, involves the step-by-step integration and testing of modules or module groups. This can be further categorized into:

    - Top-Down: Initiates testing from the highest-level modules, gradually moving to lower-level modules, employing stubs for simulating not-yet-integrated lower modules.

    - Bottom-Up: Starts with the lowest-level modules and progresses upwards, utilizing drivers to replicate the behavior of higher-level modules pending integration.

    - Hybrid (Sandwich): Merges the top-down and bottom-up methods, facilitating concurrent testing of the system's upper and lower segments.

3. Continuous Integration: Particularly in agile development settings, continuous integration involves the regular merging and testing of changes, often through automation, to maintain ongoing system integrity and functionality.

Recommended Practices for Integration Testing

- Early Integration Testing Planning: Outline the integration testing approach during the initial stages of development to identify integration points and dependencies clearly.

- Comprehensive Test Case Development: Formulate detailed test cases covering all potential component interactions, including unusual cases and failure scenarios.

- Employment of Test Harnesses and Tools: Utilize test harnesses, along with drivers and stubs, for emulating the functionality of yet-to-be-integrated modules. Apply automation tools and frameworks for integration testing where feasible.

- Controlled Test Environment Maintenance: Ensure the testing environment closely replicates the production setting yet remains isolated to prevent disruptions to ongoing development or live systems.

- Focus on Key Integration Paths: Concentrate initial testing efforts on vital paths and functionalities to optimize the impact of early testing phases.

- Diligent Test Result Monitoring: Consistently observe test executions, scrutinizing outcomes to swiftly identify and rectify issues. Document insights and refine testing strategies as necessary.

Conclusion

Integration testing is indispensable in validating the seamless operation of an application's interconnected modules. By leveraging strategic testing methods and adhering to established best practices, development teams can effectively uncover and remedy integration-related issues, thereby augmenting the software's overall functionality and robustness. As software architectures grow in complexity, the significance of adept integration testing becomes ever more pronounced, highlighting the necessity for meticulously planned, comprehensive, and adaptable testing strategies. Keeping pace with the evolving landscape of testing techniques and tools is essential for teams committed to delivering sophisticated, high-quality software products.

Chapter Eleven

Deploying Flask Applications

Overview of deployment options

Deployment marks a pivotal phase in the journey of software development, transitioning applications from development stages to user accessibility. The deployment landscape offers a spectrum of strategies, each influencing key factors such as application reachability, efficiency, adaptability, and upkeep. Advances in cloud technologies and DevOps methodologies have broadened the array of deployment choices, accommodating diverse project specifications, organizational structures, and tech frameworks. This narrative outlines the predominant deployment methodologies, including conventional in-house hosting, deployments facilitated by cloud services, and the utilization of container technologies, along with guiding principles for selecting an apt deployment route.

Conventional In-House Hosting

In-house hosting entails the operation of applications on an organization's own infrastructure, granting unparalleled control over the computing environment for custom setups and direct oversight of security and compliance measures.

Pros

- Unrestricted Control: Grants organizations full governance over their infrastructure, enabling specific customizations and enhancements.

- Direct Oversight of Compliance and Security: Simplifies meeting particular regulatory and compliance demands through in-house management of all infrastructure and data handling aspects.

Cons

- Considerable Upfront Investment: Necessitates a significant initial financial outlay for hardware, software licenses, and infrastructure establishment.

- Ongoing Infrastructure Management: Demands continuous infrastructure maintenance, updates, and scalability adjustments, requiring a dedicated IT team and resources.

Cloud-Enabled Deployments

Cloud deployments leverage the infrastructures of cloud service providers to host applications, offering varied service models such as IaaS, PaaS, and SaaS, each providing different control levels and abstraction degrees.

Pros

- Scalability with Ease: Facilitates straightforward resource scaling in response to demand fluctuations without physical infrastructure alterations.

- Cost-Effective Model: The pay-as-you-go pricing structure diminishes initial expenses, transitioning capital expenditure to operational spending.

- Worldwide Accessibility: Ensures high application availability and global access due to the extensive networks of cloud providers.

Cons

- Dependence on Service Providers: Reliance on cloud providers may lead to potential vendor lock-in and a reduction in control over intricate infrastructure details.

- Data Security Concerns: External data storage prompts questions regarding data protection and adherence to regulatory standards.

Container Technologies and Microservices

Containerization encapsulates applications and their dependencies within containers, offering consistent environments across various stages from development to production. When paired with microservices architecture, it enables the deployment of scalable and manageable service components.

Pros

- Uniformity Across Environments: Containers assure application uniformity, alleviating discrepancies across different environments.

- Optimized Resource Usage: Containers' lightweight nature and shared kernel model promote efficient resource utilization, surpassing traditional virtual machines.

- Facilitation of CI/CD Processes: Containers naturally align with continuous integration and continuous deployment pipelines, endorsing automated testing and deployment routines.

Cons

- Management Complexity: The orchestration of numerous containers and microservices can introduce considerable complexity.

- Security Measures: The shared kernel architecture necessitates vigilant security protocols to isolate and safeguard containers.

Serverless Frameworks

Serverless architectures further abstract server management, permitting developers to concentrate on coding while cloud providers dynamically manage resource allocations.

Pros

- Simplified Operations: Removes the burdens of server management, enabling a focus on developing application functionalities.

- Efficiency in Cost: Billing based on actual resource consumption and execution times can offer cost benefits for irregular workloads.

Cons

- Startup Delays: Initialization delays (cold starts) can affect performance, particularly for sporadic workloads.

- Constrained Control: High abstraction levels can limit control over the execution environment, posing challenges for intricate or customized applications.

Deployment Strategy Selection

Identifying a suitable deployment strategy entails evaluating:

- Application Demands: Assess the specific requirements of the application, including scalability, performance, and availability.

- Financial Considerations: Review budget constraints and total ownership costs associated with various deployment models.

- Compliance Requirements: Factor in any regulatory or compliance obligations that influence data residency or security standards.

- Institutional Competency: Gauge the organization's technical prowess and ability to manage the selected deployment infrastructure.

Conclusion

The deployment domain presents a range of options, from traditional on-premises setups to modern cloud-based and serverless configurations. Each alternative brings unique benefits and challenges, necessitating careful contemplation of the application's requisites, organizational capacity, and strategic ambitions. Grasping the subtleties of diverse deployment strategies empowers organizations to make informed choices that resonate with their operational demands and overarching objectives, facilitating the successful deployment and sustained management of software solutions amidst an ever-evolving tech landscape.

Deploying to a virtual private server

Deploying applications on a Virtual Private Server (VPS) has emerged as a favored strategy for developers who desire the control and scalability akin to that of dedicated servers but at a more economical price point. A VPS operates within a shared physical server yet offers segregated environments for each user through virtualization technology, granting dedicated resources and complete administrative autonomy. This discourse aims to elucidate the deployment process on a VPS, its inherent benefits, and pivotal considerations, offering a thorough guide for developers contemplating this deployment avenue.

Insights into VPS Deployment

Occupying a segment of a physical server, a VPS is distinguished by its capacity to simulate an independent server environment for each user, courtesy of virtualization. Each segment operates with its distinct OS, resources, and configurations, striking a balance between the cost-effectiveness of shared hosting and the exclusive nature of dedicated servers.

Hallmarks of VPS Deployment

- Administrative Command: Users gain full root access, permitting the tailoring of the server environment to the application's precise requirements.

- Allocated Resources: A VPS comes with dedicated CPU, memory, and storage, ensuring stable and predictable application performance.

- Flexibility in Scaling: The VPS structure allows for resource adjustments in response to the application's evolving needs, supporting both growth and variable workloads.

Deployment Workflow on a VPS

The journey to deploying an application on a VPS spans several stages, from selecting a suitable provider to the final application launch:

1. Provider Selection: Assess VPS providers based on criteria like performance, uptime reliability, customer support, and cost structure. Renowned providers include Amazon EC2, DigitalOcean Droplets, and Linode.

2. Server Initialization: Post-provisioning, access the VPS via SSH to install the operating system, essential software, and configure the server according to the application's needs.

3. Application Deployment: Transfer the application files to the VPS, configure databases, and set up web servers (Apache, Nginx) to host the application.

4. Enhancing Security: Fortify the server with firewalls, update protocols, and secure access measures to safeguard against potential security threats.

5. Ongoing Oversight and Upkeep: Employ monitoring tools to keep tabs on server and application health, and establish routines for updates and backups.

Benefits of Opting for VPS Deployment

- Economic Efficiency: VPS deployment offers a middle ground with dedicated resources and scalability at a lower cost compared to dedicated servers.

- Tailored Server Environment: Root access enables the precise configuration of the server to align with the application's operational demands.

- Enhanced Isolation and Security: The segregated nature of a VPS improves security and mitigates the risk of resource competition among tenants.

- Consistent Performance: The guarantee of dedicated resources by reputable providers ensures steady application performance.

Critical Considerations in VPS Deployment

- Requirement for Technical Acumen: Effective VPS management demands a degree of proficiency in server administration and troubleshooting.

- Security Accountability: With greater control comes the heightened responsibility to implement and maintain security best practices.

- Potential Scalability Boundaries: Despite the scalability of VPS, physical server limitations and provider offerings might necessitate eventual migration to more expansive solutions, such as cloud services.

Deployment Best Practices on a VPS

- Prudent Provider Choice: Opt for a VPS provider that aligns with the application's geographical presence, performance needs, and support requirements.

- Server Optimization: Customize the server setup to optimize performance, removing non-essential services and fine-tuning configurations.

- Comprehensive Security Protocols: Prioritize server security through stringent firewall settings, secure SSH protocols, and regular updates.

- Consistent Monitoring and Backup Regimes: Implement systematic monitoring for performance metrics and automate backup processes to ensure data preservation and swift recovery in adverse scenarios.

Conclusion

Leveraging a Virtual Private Server for application deployment offers a harmonious blend of affordability, autonomy, and resource dedication. By navigating the deployment intricacies, capitalizing on the VPS advantages, and addressing associated challenges, developers can effectively harness this platform for their application's hosting needs. Observing best practices in provider selection, server customization, security, and maintenance underpins the successful and efficient deployment and ongoing management of applications on a

VPS. Keeping abreast of evolving virtualization technologies and server management strategies remains imperative for developers keen on refining their deployment methodologies in the dynamic landscape of software development.

Using platforms like Heroku and AWS

In today's dynamic software deployment arena, platforms such as Heroku and Amazon Web Services (AWS) are distinguished for their robust capabilities, adaptability, and user-centric designs, serving a broad spectrum of deployment requisites from nascent startups to expansive corporations. These platforms mitigate the intricacies tied to infrastructure oversight, affording developers the latitude to concentrate on crafting and enhancing applications. This exposition ventures into the deployment nuances on Heroku and AWS, elucidating their principal attributes, merits, and pivotal aspects to aid developers in making judicious decisions regarding their deployment paradigms.

Heroku: Streamlining Application Deployment

Heroku, recognized for its cloud Platform as a Service (PaaS) offering, is celebrated for its straightforwardness and emphasis on enhancing developer workflows. It masks the complexity of infrastructure management, facilitating effortless deployment, administration, and scaling of applications.

Heroku's Distinctive Attributes

- Ease of Use: Heroku's intuitive dashboard and concise command-line tools simplify application deployment and lifecycle management.

- Buildpacks Mechanism: Leveraging buildpacks, Heroku automates the build process across various programming environments, ensuring versatility.

- Extensive Add-ons Marketplace: A comprehensive array of add-ons provides integrated services such as data storage, monitoring, and email services, enriching application functionality.

- Dynos - The Execution Units: Applications on Heroku are executed within dynos - lightweight, scalable containers that can be dynamically adjusted to meet traffic demands.

Merits of Opting for Heroku

- Accelerated Deployment: Heroku's streamlined platform accelerates the deployment process, enabling rapid application launch.

- Infrastructure Management: The platform's managed nature frees developers from the nuances of infrastructure upkeep, focusing on development.

- Scalability: Heroku supports both vertical and horizontal scaling, ensuring applications can grow and adapt to user demand seamlessly.

Heroku Considerations

- Scaling Costs: While Heroku is economical for smaller applications, costs can escalate as applications expand and necessitate additional resources.

- Platform Constraints: The managed platform nature introduces certain limitations on customization and direct infrastructure control.

AWS: Comprehensive Cloud Solutions

Amazon Web Services encapsulates an exhaustive suite of cloud services, from computing and storage capabilities to advanced analytics and artificial intelligence, supporting a vast array of application needs and complexities.

AWS's Core Features

- Broad Service Spectrum: AWS's extensive range of services caters to diverse application requirements, from foundational computing resources to cutting-edge machine learning tools.

- Global Infrastructure Network: Its worldwide data center footprint ensures applications have high availability and reduced latency.

- Resource Scalability: AWS allows for real-time resource scaling, aligning with application demands efficiently.

Advantages of AWS Deployment

- Versatility: The wide-ranging services and infrastructure make AWS suitable for a myriad of applications, from smaller ventures to complex enterprise solutions.

- In-depth Customization: AWS grants detailed control over the cloud environment, enabling precise resource optimization and configuration.

- Innovative Edge: AWS consistently integrates the latest technological advancements into its platform, maintaining a leading edge in cloud solutions.

AWS Deployment Considerations

- Operational Complexity: Navigating AWS's vast array of services and configurations can be daunting, necessitating a comprehensive understanding of cloud architectures.

- Cost Oversight: The pay-as-you-go pricing model, while flexible, requires vigilant management to optimize expenditures and avoid unnecessary costs.

Navigating the Choice Between Heroku and AWS

Deciding between Heroku and AWS involves evaluating various factors such as application complexity, customization needs, budgetary constraints, and team's technical proficiency:

- Heroku shines for those prioritizing ease of deployment, streamlined management, and are operating small to medium-sized applications.

- AWS caters to a broader range of applications, demanding extensive customization, scalability, and a suite of specialized services, suitable for both small and intricate, large-scale systems.

Conclusion

Heroku and Amazon Web Services have revolutionized the deployment landscape, offering scalable and flexible solutions that cater to diverse application deployment needs. Heroku's simplicity and focus on developer experience make it an excellent choice for straightforward deployment and management, while AWS's comprehensive suite of services and granular control cater to a wide range of applications, from simple web apps to complex systems. Understanding the unique features, advantages, and considerations of each platform enables developers to select the most appropriate environment for their applications, aligning with project requirements, budget, and expertise. Staying abreast of developments in platforms like Heroku and AWS is crucial for leveraging cloud-based deployment strategies effectively.

Chapter Twelve

Best Practices for Flask Development

Structuring Flask projects for scalability

Designing Flask projects with scalability in mind is essential for developers who envision their applications evolving to meet increasing user demands and expanding functionalities. Flask, recognized for its straightforwardness and adaptability as a Python-based micro web framework, requires a strategic approach to project organization to ensure long-term maintainability and scalability. This discourse delves into effective strategies for structuring Flask projects, emphasizing the significance of a well-organized codebase for enhancing scalability, facilitating collaborative development, and streamlining maintenance.

The Significance of Scalable Architecture

A scalable architecture is pivotal for accommodating growth in features, user base, and integrations seamlessly, minimizing the need for extensive rewrites. It also simplifies collaboration by demarcating clear code organization and responsibilities.

Essential Elements of a Scalable Flask Project

A scalable Flask project typically encompasses several critical elements:

- Application Factory: Serves as the nucleus for Flask app instantiation, enabling configurable setups tailored for various environments like development, testing, and production.

- Blueprints: Facilitate application modularization by clustering related functionalities, promoting code reusability and minimizing interdependencies.

- Models: Dedicated modules or packages for data models encapsulate database schemas and core business logic.

- Forms: Manages user input handling and validation, often employing Flask extensions to enhance functionality and security.

- Templates: Hosts Jinja2-powered HTML templates for dynamic content rendering within the user interface.

- Static Assets: Stores unchanging frontend assets such as CSS, JavaScript, and images.

- Configuration Management: Centralizes application settings, distinguishing between various operational environments for streamlined configuration adjustments.

- Extensions Initialization: Allocates a space for initializing and configuring Flask extensions to augment application capabilities.

- Testing Suite: Incorporates tests to ensure code reliability, leveraging Flask's testing capabilities for simulating request-response cycles.

Structuring Best Practices for Flask Projects

- Adopt Clear Naming Standards: Employ unambiguous and consistent naming for enhanced code clarity and navigability.

- Implement the Application Factory Pattern: Utilize an application factory for Flask app creation, offering flexibility in configuration and simplifying testing setups.

- Embrace Modular Design with Blueprints: Utilize blueprints for functional compartmentalization, aiding in application extensibility and maintenance.

- Practice Separation of Concerns: Maintain a clear distinction between data models, business logic, and presentation layers to improve code organization.

- Centralize Configuration Settings: Manage application configurations from a singular point, facilitating seamless environment-specific adjustments.

- Utilize Flask Extensions: Integrate Flask extensions to introduce functionalities like ORM, authentication, and form handling efficiently.

- Prioritize Comprehensive Testing: Embed testing within the development process, ensuring all components are rigorously validated for robustness.

- Incorporate Version Control: Leverage version control systems for organized feature development, bug fixes, and release management.

Enhancing Scalability through Extensions and Services

To bolster scalability, Flask projects can integrate with a range of Flask extensions and external services:

- Database Scalability Solutions: Adopt Flask-SQLAlchemy for ORM capabilities and seamless database migrations, supporting data layer scalability.

- Caching Mechanisms: Apply Flask-Caching to enhance response efficiency and reduce server load.

- Asynchronous Task Handling: Employ task queues like Celery to manage background operations and distribute processing loads.

- Traffic Management: Utilize load balancers and reverse proxies to evenly distribute incoming traffic, ensuring high availability and system resilience.

Conclusion

Carefully structuring Flask projects is paramount for ensuring they can gracefully scale alongside growing demands and expanding functionalities. By following structured best practices, such as leveraging blueprints for modularity, maintaining a clear separation of concerns, and harnessing the power of Flask extensions, developers can create robust, scalable applications. Incorporating elements like comprehensive testing, scalable database solutions, and version control is crucial for sustaining application growth and adaptability. As the Flask ecosystem continues to thrive, embracing these structured approaches remains essential for developers looking to build dynamic, scalable web applications.

Security considerations and best practices

In the current era where digital threats are on the rise, integrating strong security protocols into software applications is paramount. This approach is vital for protecting sensitive information, ensuring user trust, and complying with legal standards. This narrative examines essential security facets and introduces foundational practices that developers and enterprises should incorporate to shield their applications from emerging vulnerabilities and security infringements.

Primary Security Facets

1. Ensuring Data Privacy: The essence of application security lies in the safeguarding of stored and transmitted data. Implementing encryption methodologies like TLS for data in transit and AES for stored data guarantees the security and privacy of critical information.

2. Strengthening User Verification: Establishing solid authentication and access management systems is crucial for confirming user identities and regulating their access to specific application areas and functionalities according to their roles.

3. Stringent Input Checks: To counteract prevalent threats such as SQL injection, XSS, and command injection, it's imperative to thoroughly examine and cleanse all user inputs, eliminating the risk of hostile code execution.

4. Securing User Sessions: Defending against session-related vulnerabilities necessitates robust session management protocols, including the deployment of

secure session identifiers and enacting session expiry mechanisms.

5. Strategic Error Handling: Tailoring error responses to prevent the exposition of sensitive system insights through error messages is vital for masking potential avenues of attack.

6. Keeping Dependencies Updated: Regularly refreshing dependencies and third-party libraries to their most secure releases is crucial for addressing security weaknesses present in older versions.

Foundational Security Practices

- Prioritizing Security Early On: Embedding security considerations at the onset of the software development lifecycle, encompassing threat modeling and security evaluations during the design phase, fosters a security-centric culture.

- Enforcing Minimal Access Rights: Limiting user and system access privileges to the absolute necessities minimizes the potential impact of compromised accounts or systems.

- Complying with Secure Coding Guidelines: Observing secure coding standards, such as those proposed in OWASP's Top Ten, and employing code scrutiny and analysis tools are essential for spotting and amending security flaws.

- Enhancing Access Control Mechanisms: Bolstering access controls with multi-factor authentication (MFA) and implementing comprehensive authorization frameworks like OAuth and RBAC strengthens the application's defense against unauthorized entries.

- API Security Enforcement: Given the critical role of APIs in accessing vital data and functionalities, securing them with stringent authentication, input validation, and usage limitations is essential.

- Encryption of Sensitive Information: Applying robust encryption for data at rest and in motion, alongside secure password storage practices, is fundamental for information security.

- Utilizing Security Headers: The deployment of HTTP security headers significantly boosts security by guiding browsers on securely processing the site's content.

- Routine Security Assessments: Regular security checks, including penetration tests and vulnerability scans, aid in early detection and rectification of security issues. Embedding automated security evaluations into the CI/CD pipeline ensures ongoing security monitoring.

- Ongoing Security Awareness: Keeping abreast of the latest security threats and solutions is crucial. Continuous security education for development teams fosters an environment of security mindfulness.

- Crafting an Incident Management Plan: Formulating a detailed incident response strategy enables prompt and efficient action in the face of a security breach, reducing damage and expediting recovery.

Conclusion

In a landscape marked by frequent cyber occurrences, elevating application security from a mere best practice to an indispensable norm is essential. By addressing critical security concerns and instituting robust best practices, developers and organizations can significantly fortify their application's security framework. Adopting a proactive stance on security not only safeguards vital data and infrastructures but also strengthens stakeholder confidence. As the realm of cyber threats continues to expand, adapting and evolving security strategies and practices is necessary to navigate the complexities of cybersecurity effectively.

Performance optimization tips

Enhancing performance within software development and systems management is crucial, impacting user engagement, resource efficiency, and system functionality. In today's fast-paced digital environment, achieving and maintaining high-performance levels in applications is not just beneficial but essential. This discussion provides an array of strategies for optimizing performance across the technology stack, including best practices in coding, database management, server setup, and front-end improvements.

Optimization in Code Development

1. Choosing Algorithms and Structures Wisely: Selecting the right algorithms and data structures can significantly affect application efficiency. Opt for those

with minimal computational requirements that suit the task at hand.

2. Code Optimization and Streamlining: Using profiling tools to detect slow code sections and refining these areas can enhance application speed and decrease memory usage.

3. Implementing Asynchronous Techniques: For operations dependent on input/output, asynchronous methods ensure the application remains active, optimizing usage of system resources.

4. Adopting Effective Caching Strategies: Caching commonly accessed data can avoid repetitive and resource-intensive operations, enhancing overall performance.

Database Interaction Enhancements

1. Optimizing Indexes: Proper indexing can dramatically improve database query speeds. Regularly review and optimize indexes based on the most frequent and critical queries.

2. Query Refinement: Craft queries to minimize data fetching and reduce reliance on resource-heavy operations, enhancing efficiency.

3. Connection Pooling Usage: Employing connection pooling reduces the overhead associated with creating new database connections, beneficial in scenarios with high request volumes.

4. Database Structure Optimization: While normalizing databases reduces redundancy, some scenarios might benefit from denormalization to speed up read operations.

Server Configuration and Infrastructure Adjustments

1. Implementing Load Balancing: Distributing incoming traffic across several servers via load balancers can prevent any single server from becoming overwhelmed, improving responsiveness and system robustness.

2. Scalability Planning: Architecting systems with scalability in focus ensures that they can grow seamlessly, accommodating increased loads without significant reconfiguration.

3. Dynamic Resource Allocation: Monitoring system resource usage and adjusting allocations based on demand can prevent bottlenecks, with cloud-based auto-scaling offering an automated solution.

4. Leveraging CDNs for Content Delivery: Utilizing CDNs for serving static assets can reduce latency and accelerate content delivery to users worldwide.

Client-Facing Enhancements

1. Streamlining and Compressing Assets: Minifying and compressing CSS, JavaScript, and HTML files reduce their size, speeding up loading times.

2. Image Optimization Practices: Employing compression and modern formats for images, alongside lazy loading

techniques, can improve page load speeds without sacrificing quality.

3. HTTP Request Reduction: Consolidating resources and minimizing external library use can decrease the number of HTTP requests, further optimizing loading times.

4. Maximizing Browser Caching: Configuring caching for static resources guides browsers on how long to store these assets, reducing load times on subsequent visits.

Sustaining Optimal Performance

- Persistent Performance Monitoring: Establishing a comprehensive system for monitoring both backend and frontend performance, including real user metrics, is key to understanding and improving application behavior.

- Consistent Performance Evaluations: Regular performance audits with tools like Lighthouse or WebPageTest, integrated into the development cycle, help in identifying and rectifying performance regressions.

- Staying Informed and Updated: Keeping software dependencies and tools current ensures access to the latest performance optimizations and features.

Conclusion

Optimizing performance is a multi-faceted endeavor, requiring attention to detail across all layers of an application, from backend code efficiency and database operations to server configurations and frontend interactions. By implementing the outlined strategies and maintaining a cycle of continuous evaluation and improvement, development teams can significantly boost application performance. As the digital landscape evolves, staying updated on emerging performance optimization techniques and tools is critical to keeping applications fast, efficient, and scalable in a competitive digital ecosystem.

Chapter Thirteen

Beyond the Basics

Introduction to more advanced Flask features

Flask, a compact yet powerful Python web framework, is widely appreciated for its straightforward approach, making it an excellent option for developing small to mid-sized web projects. Beyond its basic functionalities, Flask extends its utility with a suite of advanced features and extensions that cater to more intricate development requirements, thereby enhancing an application's scalability, security, and overall capabilities. This exposition sheds light on several of these sophisticated Flask features, illustrating how they can be employed to construct comprehensive, high-performance web solutions.

Leveraging Application Factories and Blueprints

The application factory pattern in Flask facilitates the creation of Flask app instances with distinct configurations, ideal for tailoring settings for various environments like development, testing, and production. Complementing this, Blueprints enable the segregation of the application into discrete modules, each housing its routes, templates, and assets, thereby promoting reusability and modular organization.

Database Connectivity and ORM Integration

Flask's adaptability shines with its capacity to integrate with ORM extensions such as Flask-SQLAlchemy for relational databases and Flask-MongoEngine for NoSQL databases. These integrations abstract database operations into Pythonic classes and objects, simplifying database interactions and boosting development efficiency.

Form Management with Flask-WTF

Flask-WTF enhances form handling within Flask, streamlining form creation, data validation, and CSRF protection. This integration simplifies managing user submissions and file uploads, ensuring secure and efficient data handling.

Implementing Authentication and Authorization

Extensions like Flask-Login and Flask-Principal fortify Flask applications with robust user authentication and role-based access control mechanisms. Flask-Login manages user session management, whereas Flask-Principal allows for detailed permissions and access controls based on user roles.

Building RESTful APIs with Flask-RESTful

Flask-RESTful promotes the development of RESTful web services, offering a structured approach to API construction in Flask. It simplifies resource routing and request parsing, aligning with REST architectural principles for API design.

Real-time Communications via Flask-SocketIO

For applications necessitating real-time interactions, Flask-SocketIO introduces WebSocket support, enabling live, two-way communication channels between the server and clients, ideal for features like instant messaging and live updates.

Asynchronous Task Management with Celery

Celery integration allows Flask applications to handle long-running operations asynchronously, such as sending batch emails or processing extensive data, enhancing the application's responsiveness and user experience.

Enhancing Performance with Flask-Caching

The Flask-Caching extension offers caching capabilities, supporting multiple backends and significantly reducing response times by caching commonly requested data and computation-heavy operations.

Supporting Multilingual Applications with Flask-Babel

Flask-Babel equips Flask applications with internationalization (i18n) and localization (l10n) support, facilitating the translation of applications into various languages and customizing applications for different regional settings.

Extending Functionality with Custom CLI Commands

Flask's provision for custom command-line interface (CLI) commands enables developers to perform administrative tasks efficiently, from database migrations to system diagnostics.

Advanced Testing and Debugging Tools

Flask's built-in testing client and debugger aid in application testing and troubleshooting. Additional tools like Flask-Testing provide extended functionalities for comprehensive testing, ensuring application reliability.

Conclusion

While Flask is celebrated for its simplicity, its advanced functionalities and rich ecosystem of extensions empower developers to tackle complex web development challenges. By harnessing features like application factories, blueprints, ORM support, sophisticated authentication, RESTful API construction, real-time communication capabilities, and more, developers can craft scalable, secure, and feature-laden web applications. As Flask's development landscape continues to evolve, embracing these advanced features and practices is crucial for developers aiming to fully leverage Flask's potential in delivering top-tier web solutions.

Building larger applications with Flask Blueprints

Developing expansive applications with Flask calls for an architecture that can gracefully handle increasing complexity while maintaining efficiency and ease of upkeep. Flask Blueprints serve as an essential tool in this regard, offering a structured approach to segmenting applications into modular, independently manageable components. This exploration delves into the Flask Blueprints mechanism, highlighting its critical role in crafting larger-scale applications and providing insights into best practices for its optimal deployment.

The Role of Flask Blueprints

Flask Blueprints function as subcomponents or mini-applications within the broader Flask application framework, facilitating the organized grouping of functionalities, routes, and views. They enable a more structured and compartmentalized approach to application development.

Advantages of Blueprints in Complex Applications

1. Modular Design: Blueprints enable the division of applications into discrete modules, each focused on a specific set of functionalities, thus enhancing code clarity and maintenance.

2. Code Reusability: Defined within Blueprints, components can be effortlessly repurposed across various application sections or even across different projects, adhering to DRY principles.

3. Application Growth Management: The modular nature of Blueprints simplifies the process of scaling and evolving applications, allowing for the addition or modification of modules with minimal impact on the broader application framework.

4. Collaborative Development Efficiency: Blueprints allow development teams to work on distinct application segments concurrently, streamlining development workflows and simplifying integration.

Flask Blueprints: Best Practice Guidelines

- Strategic Blueprint Organization: Align Blueprints with logical application segments, such as user management, administration interfaces, or service features, to facilitate navigation and comprehension of the application's structure.

- Unified Configuration Approach: Despite Blueprints' capacity for localized configurations, maintaining a centralized configuration setup for the overarching application ensures uniformity and streamlined management.

- Mindful Blueprint Registration: Thoughtfully register Blueprints with the Flask application object, considering the use of application factories for flexible application initialization and Blueprint registration tailored to specific contexts.

- URL Prefixing Consistency: Employ URL prefixes judiciously when registering Blueprints to prevent routing conflicts and to clearly delineate the scope of Blueprint routes within the application's URL schema.

- Organized Template Management: Establish a coherent structure and naming convention for Blueprint-associated templates to prevent naming overlaps and promote an organized template architecture.

- Blueprint-Specific Static Assets: When Blueprints encompass unique static files, ensure these assets are correctly referenced in templates and appropriately served by Flask.

- Loose Coupling Between Blueprints: Facilitate inter-Blueprint communication through Flask's application context and signaling mechanisms, preserving component independence.

- Independent Blueprint Testing: Conduct tests for individual Blueprint components in isolation and within the full application context to ensure component integrity and functionality.

Blueprint Integration with Flask Extensions

Flask Blueprints seamlessly integrate with various Flask extensions, allowing each Blueprint to utilize functionalities provided by extensions such as Flask-SQLAlchemy, Flask-Login, and Flask-WTF, while maintaining a clear separation from the extension initialization process.

Blueprint Utilization Patterns

- Appropriate Applications: Blueprints excel in structuring distinct application areas, API version management, and admin interface development, where their encapsulation and organizational benefits are most pronounced.

- Caution Against Excessive Fragmentation: While Blueprints promote modularity, over-segmentation can introduce undue complexity. It's crucial to find a balance that fosters both modularity and simplicity.

Blueprint Deployment in Practice

In real-world scenarios, Blueprints prove instrumental across a spectrum of Flask applications, from mid-size projects with separate user and administrative functionalities to large-scale systems with intricate business logic. They are employed in diverse domains such as e-commerce, content management, and API services, showcasing the adaptability and efficacy of Blueprints in facilitating structured and scalable web application development.

Conclusion

Blueprints emerge as a cornerstone in the architecture of larger Flask applications, providing the frameworks for modularization, scalability, and streamlined maintenance. Adhering to established best practices in the organization, registration, and utilization of Blueprints empowers developers to leverage their full potential in constructing sophisticated, feature-rich applications. As the demands on applications grow, the strategic employment of Blueprints remains integral to navigating the complexities of large-scale application development with agility and precision.

Leveraging Flask's signals and middleware

Utilizing signals and middleware within Flask applications presents an effective avenue for augmenting functionality, refining code structure, and managing request-response workflows adeptly. This narrative ventures into the realms of Flask signals and middleware, shedding light on their functionalities, practical applications, and the principles for their judicious deployment in Flask-based development endeavors.

Grasping Flask Signals

Flask signals offer a robust mechanism akin to the observer pattern, enabling the execution of custom logic in reaction to specific occurrences within the Flask application lifecycle. These occurrences encompass a wide array of events from the onset of a request to the finalization of a response, providing pivotal junctures for the integration of custom operations.

Practical Utilizations of Flask Signals

1. Logging Events: Employ signals for the meticulous logging of pivotal events, such as user authentication actions, errors during requests, or alterations in configurations, aiding in the troubleshooting and oversight of the application.

2. Monitoring User Interactions: Leverage request-related signals for delineating user activities, offering valuable insights for analytical assessments and understanding user engagement patterns.

3. Managing Resources: Utilize signals associated with request completion or application cessation for the orderly release of resources, ensuring the seamless termination of database connections or ancillary services.

4. Automating Notifications: Harness specific application events to trigger automated communications, such as emails or alerts, fostering enhanced interaction and engagement with users.

Principles for Flask Signals Utilization

- Judicious Signal Engagement: Engage with signals thoughtfully, concentrating on events critical to the application's operational or monitoring needs to mitigate unnecessary performance overhead.

- Logic Segregation: Ensure a clear demarcation between the core application logic and the signal handling routines, promoting a modular and maintainable codebase.

- Asynchronous Execution: Where feasible, manage signals asynchronously, particularly for operations peripheral to the core request-response cycle, to preserve application responsiveness.

- Comprehensive Documentation: Meticulously document the signal handlers, elucidating the associated events and their intended functionalities, thereby enhancing code comprehensibility and maintainability.

Middleware in Flask: Interceding in Request-Response Transactions

Middleware in Flask acts as an intermediary layer capable of intercepting and manipulating both incoming requests before they reach their designated view functions and outgoing responses prior to their dispatch to clients. This intermediary layer is pivotal for implementing overarching concerns such as access control, logging, and modifying requests or responses.

Middleware Deployment in Flask

In Flask, middleware is typically realized by encapsulating the Flask application or specific blueprints, enabling the middleware to examine and alter requests and responses, embedding custom logic prior to or following the execution of view functions.

Middleware Applications

1. Access Control Mechanisms: Middleware can scrutinize incoming requests to enforce authentication and authorization protocols, safeguarding access to specific endpoints or resources.

2. Logging and Surveillance: Capture intricate details of incoming requests, facilitating application monitoring and diagnostics.

3. Altering Responses: Adapt outgoing responses by appending headers, compressing content, or adjusting status codes to align with application standards or client requisites.

4. Implementing Rate Limiting: Enforce rate limiting to regulate the volume of requests from users within defined timeframes, mitigating misuse and ensuring equitable resource distribution.

Flask Middleware Best Practices

- Non-intrusive Design: Craft middleware to minimally disrupt the request-response workflow, executing only essential tasks without introducing notable latency.

- Focus on Reusability: Construct middleware with versatility in mind, allowing for its application across varied routes, blueprints, or Flask projects.

- Customization Options: Furnish middleware with configurable parameters, enabling its adaptation based on application configurations or environmental variables.

- Robust Error Management: Incorporate comprehensive error handling within middleware to manage exceptions gracefully, preventing middleware malfunctions from affecting the overall application integrity.

Conclusion

Signals and middleware stand as formidable tools in the Flask ecosystem, enabling the enrichment of applications through event-driven actions and the strategic interception of request-response cycles. By observing established best practices in their implementation and application, developers can leverage these constructs to craft modular, scalable, and feature-enriched Flask applications. Through the strategic employment of signals for event logging and notifications, alongside middleware for request handling and access control, these functionalities empower developers to enhance both the user experience and the operational efficiency of Flask applications.

Conclusion

Recap of key concepts covered in the book

This comprehensive guide has traversed the expansive terrain of Flask, a Python-based microframework celebrated for its agility and potency in web application development. From foundational elements to the nuances of advanced functionalities, this text has endeavored to arm readers with a profound understanding and the practical acumen needed to exploit Flask's full potential in crafting sophisticated web solutions. This synopsis aims to encapsulate the pivotal themes and insights presented, fostering an integrated comprehension and facilitating their pragmatic application in Flask-driven projects.

Core Flask Principles

- Initial Flask Setup and Configurations: The journey commenced with the essentials of establishing a Flask environment, accentuating the significance of a methodical project architecture and the adoption of environment-specific configurations to adeptly manage settings across development, testing, and production stages.

- Dynamic Routing and Views: We delved into Flask's routing mechanisms that associate URLs to Python functions, elaborating on the creation of dynamic routes and the adept handling of various HTTP methods to cater to client requests.

- Dynamic Content with Templates: Utilizing Jinja2 for dynamic HTML content rendering was explored, alongside strategies for the organization and delivery of static assets like CSS and JavaScript, enriching the user interface and interaction.

Managing Data and User Inputs

- Database Connections: The discourse extended to Flask's compatibility with diverse databases, discussing the integration with ORM tools such as Flask-SQLAlchemy for relational databases and Flask-MongoEngine for NoSQL databases, streamlining data operations.

- Form Handling via Flask-WTF: The management of user inputs through forms, emphasizing secure data handling, validation, and CSRF protection, was examined, showcasing the integration with Flask-WTF for enhanced form operations.

Structuring and Modularizing Applications

- Leveraging Application Factories: The application factory concept was introduced for the dynamic creation of Flask app instances, promoting flexible configurations and initialization.

- Blueprints for Modular Development: The segmentation of Flask applications into independent, reusable modules using Blueprints was discussed, encouraging a cleaner, more maintainable code structure.

Advanced Functionalities in Flask

- RESTful API Construction: The book outlined the principles of developing RESTful APIs with Flask, focusing on API design, data serialization, and employing Flask-RESTful for efficient web service creation.

- Securing Applications: Topics on application security, including user authentication, session management, and role-based access controls, were covered, utilizing tools like Flask-Login and Flask-Principal.

- Asynchronous Operations and Background Tasks: The incorporation of asynchronous functionalities and background task execution in Flask, particularly through Celery integration, was explored to boost application responsiveness.

Enhancing Performance and Scalability

- Implementing Caching Mechanisms: Approaches to caching were discussed to mitigate server load and enhance response times, with an emphasis on Flask-Caching and related techniques.

- Scalability Strategies: The narrative addressed scalability strategies for Flask applications, from deploying load balancers to utilizing CDNs, ensuring the application's capability to handle growing traffic volumes.

Emphasizing Security and Robustness

- Application Security Practices: The paramount importance of securing Flask applications was highlighted, discussing practices to mitigate vulnerabilities and ensure encrypted communications via HTTPS.

Testing and Launching Applications

- Rigorous Application Testing: The critical role of testing was emphasized, detailing practices for unit and integration testing to ensure comprehensive coverage and application reliability.

- Deployment Considerations: The text concluded with insights into deployment strategies for Flask applications, from utilizing WSGI servers like Gunicorn to containerization with Docker, and cloud deployments on platforms such as Heroku and AWS.

Conclusion

Navigating through the Flask framework, this text has presented a thorough examination of its capabilities, preparing readers to develop web applications that are not only functional but also secure, scalable, and maintainable. By revisiting these fundamental concepts and judiciously applying them, developers are well-equipped to leverage Flask's flexibility and efficiency in their web development endeavors. Engaging with the ongoing developments within the Flask community will further refine and enhance one's expertise in this versatile framework.

Resources for further learning and development

Pursuing continuous education and skill enhancement is essential for individuals in the rapidly changing tech industry. The pursuit of advanced knowledge and skills requires access to a variety of educational resources designed to deepen understanding, refine abilities, and keep up with the latest technological advancements. This document outlines a range of educational avenues and platforms aimed at supporting ongoing learning and career development within the fields of technology and software engineering.

Digital Learning Platforms and Hands-on Training

1. Online Educational Portals: Prominent platforms like Coursera, edX, and Udacity offer an extensive array of courses in areas such as computer science, software engineering, and data analysis, partnering with leading academic institutions and industry experts to provide both free and premium courses.

2. Interactive Coding Platforms: Sites such as Codecademy, Khan Academy, and FreeCodeCamp offer practical coding exercises and project-based learning in various programming disciplines, suitable for learners at all levels.

3. Video Course Libraries: Resources like Udemy, Pluralsight, and LinkedIn Learning host vast collections of video tutorials and comprehensive courses on specific technologies, languages, and career skills, catering to both beginners and experienced professionals.

Reference Materials and Academic Resources

1. Core Documentation: Primary documentation for programming languages, frameworks, and tools acts as a crucial resource for mastering fundamental concepts, functionalities, and best practices straight from the primary sources.

2. API Documentation: For those working with APIs, detailed API documentation is vital for understanding the functionalities, data structures, and methods of integration.

3. Technical Blogs and Articles: Platforms such as Medium, Dev.to, and individual blogs of thought leaders in the industry often contain valuable insights, tutorials, and case studies on a wide range of technical topics.

Print and Electronic Literature

1. Specialized Technical Books: Renowned publishers like O'Reilly Media, Manning Publications, and Packt publish a broad selection of technical books authored by field experts, covering areas from programming languages to software architecture and design patterns.

2. Digital Libraries: Online resources such as Project Gutenberg and Google Books offer access to a vast collection of digital books, including both historical texts and modern works in computer science and technology.

Community Interaction and Professional Exchanges

1. Online Forums and Collaborative Platforms: Spaces like Stack Overflow, specific Reddit communities (e.g., r/programming), and GitHub Discussions provide vibrant environments for troubleshooting, knowledge sharing, and project collaboration.

2. Professional Meetups and Conferences: Engaging in local user groups, technical workshops, and international tech conferences allows for networking with peers, learning from industry leaders, and staying updated on current trends.

3. Contributing to Open Source: Active participation in open-source projects on platforms like GitHub offers practical coding experience, community feedback, and networking opportunities, enriching one's professional portfolio.

Scholarly Publications and Sector Insights

1. Research Journals: Publications such as IEEE Transactions on Software Engineering and ACM Computing Surveys feature peer-reviewed research on software development methodologies, new technologies, and theoretical aspects of computing.

2. Industry Analysis: Comprehensive reports from research organizations like Gartner provide insights into technology trends, market analyses, and future predictions, supporting informed decision-making and innovation.

Multimedia and Interactive Learning

1. Technology-focused Podcasts: Engaging podcasts like "Software Engineering Daily" and "Talk Python To Me" cover a spectrum of tech-related subjects, hosting discussions with industry practitioners and specialists.

2. Educational Webinars and Live Coding Sessions: Various tech entities and community groups conduct interactive webinars and live programming sessions, offering avenues for direct engagement and learning.

Conclusion

The landscape of educational resources for ongoing learning in technology and software engineering is rich and diverse, addressing various learning styles, proficiency levels, and professional goals. Embracing a comprehensive approach that includes engaging with online courses, foundational literature, authoritative texts, community forums, scholarly research, and audio-visual content, individuals can build a holistic and evolving knowledge base and skill set. Commitment to lifelong learning, curiosity, and active engagement with the tech community are pivotal for personal and professional advancement in the fast-paced technology sector.

Next steps in your Flask development journey

Advancing in your Flask development path offers a gateway to crafting more intricate and efficient web platforms. Moving from foundational knowledge to exploring Flask's broader capabilities marks a journey of skill enhancement, adherence to refined development methodologies, and active participation within the expansive Flask community. This outline suggests future directions and initiatives to elevate your Flask development trajectory, emphasizing skill augmentation, the adoption of development best practices, and community involvement to ensure a progressive and innovative approach to web application creation.

Elevating Flask Proficiency

1. Exploring In-depth Flask Functionalities: Venture into the more complex features of Flask, such as the strategic use of application factories for enhanced scalability, the application of blueprints for structuring expansive applications, and the effective utilization of Flask's command-line utilities. Gaining mastery over these advanced features equips you to develop sophisticated, modular web solutions.

2. Advanced Database Interaction Techniques: Enhance your capabilities in database management, focusing on sophisticated ORM strategies with Flask-SQLAlchemy and delving into Flask-MongoEngine for projects utilizing NoSQL databases. Proficient database interaction is essential for the creation of dynamic, data-driven applications.

3. Front-end Integration Skills: Broadening your expertise to include front-end technologies enhances your ability to construct comprehensive full-stack applications, thereby improving user interfaces and experiences.

Implementing Development Best Practices

1. Security as a Foremost Priority: Elevate the security measures in your Flask applications by understanding and mitigating prevalent security vulnerabilities, following the guidelines of the OWASP Top 10, and implementing critical security protocols.

2. Establishing a Rigorous Testing Framework: Develop a comprehensive approach to testing, encompassing various testing methodologies to ensure your Flask applications are reliable and free from defects.

3. Performance Tuning and Optimization: Concentrate on optimizing your Flask applications for superior performance through effective coding practices, database query optimization, and caching strategies.

Engaging with the Flask Development Community

1. Active Open Source Engagement: Immerse yourself in the Flask open-source community by contributing to Flask or its extensions, enhancing your skills and broadening your professional network.

2. Continuous Learning and Community Interaction: Remain updated with the latest in Flask and web development trends by engaging with community forums, attending conferences, and participating in meetups.

3. Disseminating Knowledge: Share your Flask experiences and insights through blogging, tutorials, or presentations, contributing to the collective knowledge pool of the Flask community.

Broadening Horizons with Complementary Technologies

1. Microservices Architecture Exploration: Investigate the principles and implementation of microservices architectures, utilizing Flask to create independent, scalable services.

2. Asynchronous Programming for Dynamic Applications: Acquire expertise in asynchronous programming and real-time communication to build more interactive applications, leveraging technologies such as WebSockets and frameworks like Celery.

3. Mastering Cloud Deployments and DevOps Practices: Gain proficiency in deploying Flask applications on cloud platforms and incorporating DevOps methodologies to enhance development efficiency and application delivery.

Real-world Project Involvement

1. Portfolio Development: Continually work on diverse projects to demonstrate your Flask capabilities, showcasing your ability to address real-world problems and adhere to development best practices.

2. Collaborative Project Participation: Engage in team projects, either within your professional circles or through open-source contributions, to expose yourself to new development practices and technologies.

Conclusion

Your journey in Flask development is characterized by continuous learning, practical application, and engagement with the broader development community. By expanding your technical knowledge, integrating best practices into your development processes, contributing to the Flask ecosystem, and applying your expertise to real-world projects, you pave the way for sustained growth and innovation in web application development. Approach each new challenge with zeal and leverage the supportive Flask community to further your development career.

Printed in Poland
by Amazon Fulfillment
Poland Sp. z o.o., Wrocław